INSIGHTS

General Editor: Clive Bloom, Middlesex University

Editorial Board: Clive Bloom, Brian Docherty, Gary Day and Lesley Bloom

Insights brings to academics, students and general readers the very best contemporary criticism on neglected literary and cultural areas. It consists of anthologies, each containing original contributions by advanced scholars and experts. Each contribution concentrates on a study of a particular work, author or genre in its artistic, historical and cultural context.

Published titles

Clive Bloom (*editor*)
JACOBEAN POETRY AND PROSE: Rhetoric, Representation and the Popular Imagination
TWENTIETH-CENTURY SUSPENSE: The Thriller Comes of Age
SPY THRILLERS: From Buchan to le Carré
AMERICAN DRAMA

Clive Bloom and Brian Docherty (*editors*)
AMERICAN POETRY: The Modernist Ideal

Clive Bloom, Brian Docherty, Jane Gibb and Keith Shand (*editors*)
NINETEENTH-CENTURY SUSPENSE: From Poe to Conan Doyle

Dennis Butts
STORIES AND SOCIETY: Children's Literature in a Social Context

Gary Day (*editor*)
READINGS IN POPULAR CULTURE: Trivial Pursuits?
THE BRITISH CRITICAL TRADITION: A Re-evaluation

Gary Day and Clive Bloom (*editors*)
PERSPECTIVES ON PORNOGRAPHY: Sexuality in Film and Literature

Brian Docherty (*editor*)
AMERICAN CRIME FICTION: Studies in the Genre
AMERICAN HORROR FICTION: From Brockden Brown to Stephen King
TWENTIETH-CENTURY EUROPEAN DRAMA

Rhys Garnett and R. J. Ellis (*editors*)
SCIENCE FICTION ROOTS AND BRANCHES: Contemporary
  Critical Approaches

Robert Giddings (*editor*)
LITERATURE AND IMPERIALISM

Robert Giddings, Keith Selby and Chris Wensley
SCREENING THE NOVEL: The Theory and Practice of Literary
  Dramatisation

Dorothy Goldman (*editor*)
WOMEN AND WORLD WAR 1: The Written Response

Graham Holderness (*editor*)
THE POLITICS OF THEATRE AND DRAMA

Paul Hyland and Neil Sammells (*editors*)
IRISH WRITING: Exile and Subversion

Maxim Jakubowski and Edward James (*editors*)
THE PROFESSION OF SCIENCE FICTION: Writers on their Craft
  and Ideas

Mark Lilly (*editor*)
LESBIAN AND GAY WRITING: An Anthology of Critical Essays

Christopher Mulvey and John Simons (*editors*)
NEW YORK: City as Text

Adrian Page (*editor*)
THE DEATH OF THE PLAYWRIGHT? Modern British Drama and
  Literary Theory

Frank Pearce and Michael Woodiwiss (*editors*)
GLOBAL CRIME CONNECTIONS: Dynamics and Control

John Simons
FROM MEDIEVAL TO MEDIEVALISM

Jeffrey Walsh and James Aulich (*editors*)
VIETNAM IMAGES: War and Representation

Gina Wisker (*editor*)
BLACK WOMEN'S WRITING

American Drama

Edited by

CLIVE BLOOM
Middlesex University

MACMILLAN

First published 1995 by
MACMILLAN PRESS LTD
Houndmills, Basingstoke, Hampshire RG21 6XS
and London
Companies and representatives
throughout the world

ISBN 0–333–53286–4 hardcover
ISBN 0–333–53287–2 paperback

A catalogue record for this book is available
from the British Library.

10   9   8   7   6   5   4   3   2   1
04   03   02   01   00   99   98   97   96   95

Printed in Great Britain by
Mackays of Chatham PLC
Chatham, Kent

Contents

Contents

Preface

American theatre hardly existed in the last century and yet in less than a hundred years America has produced one of the great stage traditions of the world. Born into this century, the drama has acted both as a reflection and as a commentary on the dominance, power and sometimes corruption of the American democratic dream.

Influenced by Ibsen and Strindberg and originating in the small theatre companies and groups of semi-professional players who gathered together in the early 1900s, this theatre has provided a fertile ground for such writers as Eugene O'Neill, Susan Glaspell, Imamu Amiri Baraka, Arthur Miller and Tennessee Williams. American theatre still challenges with a unique voice and concentration avoided by television and commercial film. It continues to deal with the issues pertinent to the 'American century' whether these be about gender, colour, political oppression or political correctness.

This volume offers a comprehensive introduction to the subject for students who require detailed but clear information on the dramatists who have been included. It also has much to offer the academic and serious reader who is involved with current debate in the area and who is concerned that the canon actively includes both the unfamiliar names and forgotten voices of those whose contribution to the history of American drama has been unfairly neglected. A range of approaches and a wide selection of examples from the plays make this volume an important contribution to the study of some of this century's greatest writers.

Acknowledgements

The editor of this volume wishes to express his gratitude to Brian Docherty without whom the present work might not exist, to Gary Day and Mike Woolf for their help and encouragement, and to Lesley Bloom for her patience.

Notes on the Contributors

Chris Banfield is a lecturer in the Department of Drama and Theatre Arts at the University of Birmingham.

Clive Bloom is currently Visiting Professor in Humanities at Luton University. His numerous books and articles range from cultural history to popular fiction.

Charlotte Canning is a Visiting Lecturer in the University of Texas at Austin Department of Theatre and Dance. She has published articles on feminism and theatre and is currently completing a book on American feminist theatre groups.

Edward J. Esche lectures at Anglia University. His research covers the Renaissance and literary theory and he is the co-author of a recent book applying the New Historicism to the sixteenth and seventeenth centuries.

Darryll Grantley teaches in the Faculty of Humanities at the University of Kent at Canterbury.

Michael J. Hayes lectures at the University of Central Lancashire and is a regular contributor to the **Insights** series.

A. Robert Lee has edited many volumes on American Literature and culture as well as being a broadcaster. He teaches at the University of Kent.

Mark Lilly teaches at the University of Monastir, Tunisia. He has served on the national executive of the National Council for Civil Liberties and is the author of several books and the editor of *Lesbian and Gay Writing* in the **Insights** series.

Eric Mottram is Emeritus Professor of English and American Literature at King's College, University of London. He has published over a dozen books on modern literature and culture including studies on William Faulkner, Allen Ginsberg and William Burroughs.

Barbara Ozieblo is a lecturer in the Departamento de Filologia Inglesa y Francesca in the Universidad de Malaga, Spain.

Michael Woolf is a writer on Anglo-American culture and is Director of the London office of the Council on International Educational Exchange.

Introduction

CLIVE BLOOM

The American serious theatre is one that has negotiated a path between the commercial optimism of Broadway and the lure of the West Coast film industry. At once experimental and avant-garde and at the same time popular and accessible, such theatre survives as a special vein of American artistic expression. Hardly immune to either Hollywood glamour or the razzmatazz of the Great White Way, this theatre has resolutely created a place of special and peculiar dramatic appeal, one uniquely stagebound. Beginning with the little theatre companies of the provinces and born into the age of jazz and movies, this 'serious' or legitimate theatre has happily found a voice acceptable to both film makers and television producers.[1] And a certain type of *apparent* adaptability has preserved its special features amongst the glitter of all-singing, all-dancing extravaganzas.

And yet, one cannot avoid a special respect for the classic form of American operetta: the musical. This theatre, written for a wide popular audience is itself a natural and peculiarly serious form of American theatrical experience; this too has thrived alongside and maybe because of Hollywood. The works of George and Ira Gershwin, Cole Porter, Rodgers and Hart, Oscar Hammerstein, Irving Berlin, Stephen Sondheim and Leonard Bernstein rank amongst the great achievements of American theatre. These alongside the work of Eugene O'Neill, Arthur Miller, Tennessee Williams, Imamu Baraka, Marsha Norman and their companions represent a theatrical experience at once alive to the popular audience and deeply imbued with its desires and fears. The musical is at once optimistic and buoyant, aware of a community of hope whilst the non-musical (with which this volume deals) seems isolated and paranoid. Here are the twin theatrical aspects of the modernity of modern American consumer society. Both were born of modernism's pulse and both are on the edge of *immediacy* and *urgency* in an age in which the total power of communal experience brings into being the

1

fragility of individual identity. Each of these theatrical forms, however, is connected to that shadow world of minstrel shows, burlesque and vaudeville which is the raw material and haunting double both of experimental theatre and Broadway musical. Here is the curiously authentic voice: immodest, intractable, vulgar, tasteless, illegitimate, risqué, that nevertheless keeps theatre aware of the risks it takes.

Such roots, fit only for denial, held to the boards the artists, writers, designers, actors and impressarios who acquiesce in the life of a greasepainted obsession and are unwilling to conform to television's anodyne nature and Hollywood's factory process, unless, and only until, both of these latter forms submit and become themselves theatrical experiences – turning into theatre and stage and denying their own conventions of film and videotape as theatre is occasionally transformed into both. To see the television or film adaptations of Arthur Miller, Tennessee Williams, Edward Albee, David Mamet, Neil Simon or Sam Shepard is to witness the intractable nature of such theatre, its very difference from film or television, except that experience is turned for the viewing audience into 'art', a *real* experience different from both film and television whose own conventions are forced to conform to the proscenium arch and glass wall of *staged* drama.

American drama bears its legitimacy and its sin with it. Thus its two greatest characters are Blanche DuBois and Gypsy Rose Lee – its hero the adulterous Willy Loman. This too is why American drama is not subsumed within television. Television cannot control the sin which is drama's art. The credibility of theatre pays out the commercialism which has paid for it. Good television drama avoids *presence*, fights shy of *immediacy*, waits for the commercial break. Television suffers from a poverty of voice and a poverty (because of a glut) of scene and gesture. Television cannot be raw – indeed it must not be so. Hollywood too engages at the level of gesture and glance – it fights shy of wordage; it avoids speech. Ideal cinema is silent – it compensates by a mobility of body and a surface both visceral and untouchable: its strength is its non-presence, blankness and lack of depth. Its own mobilised structure is formal, technical, two-dimensional, and the sexual pleasures are in the auditorium only.

The visceral, three-dimensionality of the theatrical space, at once muscular *presence* and fragile voice, is the sinful nature of raw knowledge. Unlike film and television, even and especially unlike commercial radio, the theatre offers an *authenticity* which is shocking and peculiarly distressing. This is why Hollywood and CBS need occasional shots of theatrical presence. The libido of theatre is also the adrenalin by which these other forms in America recognise themselves – by presenting what denies their conventions, lowers their viewing figures and restricts their commerciality. In theatre, the art seems preserved in speech which overrides the visual, and in a static scenario which overwhelms the mobility of the roving camera. Thus, the 'cheap' set upsets the lush production values we expect from commercial US film and television companies.

I have suggested enough for the reader to gather that the staged drama in America has created its own space between and often outside the dynamic forms of both film and television. Such a space requires our acceptance of a type of primary authenticity which unravels or questions the inauthenticity of popular consumer culture and the values of the American system. From this, however, American drama draws its inspiration (in its anti-commercial parochial origins) and its ambivalence (the commercial success of its greatest names): the Pulitzer is at once the legitimation and the insurance policy of such activity.

The age of American theatre is born of a double movement, one artistic, the other political; the former particular, the latter conditioned by a general cultural shift. It was with the influence, in the first two decades of this century, of Ibsen, Strindberg, Yeats and Nietzsche that American theatre joined the European theatre and became international. It was during the First World War that it found its voice, not international, but peculiarly American and introverted and intense, part of its own avant-garde. In a word, American theatre became international *because* of isolation and through isolationism. The appearance of H. L. Mencken's *The American Language* in 1919 marked the final legitimation of a vibrant and authentic American voice which was different from English and which was no longer secondary to English. By 1941, Mencken had revised his great work and was able, in his introduction, to point out the historical inevitability 'of the pull of American':

> But since 1923 the pull of American has become so powerful that it has begun to drag English with it, and in consequence some of the differences once visible have tended to disappear. The two forms of the language, of course, are still distinct in more ways than one, and when an Englishman and an American meet they

continue to be conscious that each speaks a tongue that is far from identical with the tongue spoken by the other. But the Englishman, of late, has yielded so much to American example, in vocabulary, in idiom, in spelling and even in pronunciation, that what he speaks promises to become, on some not too remote tomorrow, a kind of dialect of American, just as the language spoken by the American was once a dialect of English. The English writers who note this change lay it to the influence of the American movies and talkies, but it seems to me that there is also something more, and something deeper. The American people now constitute by far the largest fraction of the English-speaking race, and since the World War they have shown an increasing inclination to throw off their old subservience to English precept and example. If only by the force of numbers, they are bound to exert a dominant influence upon the course of the common language hereafter.[2]

Here, then, is that isolationism which is also international – the immediacy of *speech* overwhelms. By the 1940s America was poised to dominate the drama of the English-speaking world and the great age of American theatre was about to commence.

Yet I have already pointed out the problematic 'inauthenticity' of 'movies' and 'talkies' in the cultural agenda of the intelligentsia. Thus Mencken offers us a clue to the American drama. For the American dramatist to stake a claim to authenticity he or she must present an authentic *voice*, provide a *presence* and an *immediacy* to confront. In a word, deal in 'fact'. Movies, shopping malls, consumer society, popular culture and mass manipulation: theatre offers the dramatist a last space for the authenticity of the *individual voice*, not distanced, mediated, avoidable, but wholly, terribly there – irony of the American ideology of individual emancipation.

The dramatist provides an illusory 'truth' and a fictional fact to combat the promissory fictions of the American dream, all those broken fictional contracts promising liberty, wealth – and happiness. For such dramatists illusion is more real, overwhelming proof of the two-dollar bill handed out by Uncle Sam. Drama of this sort is restrictive, paranoid, tragic, predestined. All is consequent on a fall and grace is simply understanding. Here is individualism as heroism and tragedy. An American dream perversely celebrated in reverse and with the family as its paradigm and battleground.

The American fictions, those great dramas of expansion and of world destiny, are met head-on by the small drama of the existentialist playwright – Black, gay, feminist, Jewish, Irish. It is this drama which meets the greater fiction of national identity, meets it head-on and thrives within it. Because of it and despite it.

The theatre-goer in London in 1993 had the opportunity to see new plays by Arthur Miller and David Mamet as well as a host of revivals. This volume offers the reader a survey which not only includes classic authors such as Miller and Mamet, Williams and O'Neill, but also includes studies of the neglected playwrights Susan Glaspell and Clifford Odets, the Black Theatre of Imamu Amiri Baraka and the thriving feminist theatre of the last 30 years.

NOTES

1. Even the films of Williams, Albee and Miller are little more than filmed theatre.
2. H. L. Mencken, *The American Language* (New York: Alfred A. Knopf, 1919); extract is from the Preface to the fourth edition, 1941, p. vi.

1

Susan Glaspell

BARBARA OZIEBLO

My generation has devoted a considerable share of its labours to the recovery of early women writers: we unearthed their voice, uncovered their legacy, and so undid what was in effect a patriarchal literary canon. Recent publications, such as *American Drama: The Female Canon* and *Feminine Focus: The New Women Playwrights* testify that women's writing was not confined to the 'homely' genres of fiction and poetry, and that their writing has indeed borne fruit – for Shakespeare's sisters have now spoken out.[1]

Women's interest in the drama goes back way into pre-television days: family entertainment fell under the private sphere of home life dominated by the mother, and where her influence prevailed amateur theatricals were innocent sport. In some cases, these social events outgrew their beginnings: Anna Cora Mowatt enjoyed writing and presenting plays with her sisters and friends till, goaded by her husband's financial failure, she claimed her triumphant place on the commercial stage with *Fashion* (1845). But the theatre has never been considered merely as a source of entertainment; the ancient Festival of Dionysus had transformed religious rites and myths into art forms which evoked a powerful sense of communal identity – recognised by William Butler Yeats as a tool for political reform in Ireland. In Chicago, Jane Addams, founder of Hull House, satisfied the melancholy nostalgia of alienated and culture-starved immigrant workers when she provided them with a theatre. There, in Yeats's words, they could watch 'the sacred drama of [their] own history, every spectator finding self and neighbour, finding all the world there as we find the sun in the bright spot under the looking glass'.[2] The Hull House Players began their theatrical activities in 1899, but it was not till 1907, when they came under the direction of Laura Dainty Pelham, that they became a serious force on the little theatre scene. While they maintained their firm belief in the educational value of the theatre, they were careful not to subjugate artistic concerns to social ideals; a committed interest in native drama encouraged women such as Hilda Satt Polachek to develop her artistic talents.

In New York, the Henry Street Settlement embarked on a similar venture in 1907. Irene and Alice Lewisohn started off by producing festival plays and ritual dances with the young people of the settlement house; they ventured into spoken drama in 1911 at the Clinton Hall, and in 1915 were ready to open the Neighborhood Playhouse on Grand Street, where their audiences would experience the spiritual pulse of recovered ritual.[3] The theatre critic Kenneth MacGowan could not forgive the Players their success, for they were, he wrote, 'our one thoroughly feminist theatre'; thus he expressed no surprise at their failure in what he considered the 'rather masculine' aspect of the work of little theatres: the Neighborhood Players disappointed him because they did not specifically encourage 'the writing and production of original plays'.[4]

There was only one little theatre in the 'restless and sterile theatrical agitation' derided by Jacques Copeau in the New York of 1917 that 'dedicated itself to the experimental production of plays by American playwrights'.[5] Indeed, according to William Archer, the Provincetown venture gave birth to the modern American drama.[6] Its founder was George Cram Cook: its principal playwrights Susan Glaspell and Eugene O'Neill. The Provincetown Players went out of their way to remain unshackled by reviewers' opinions; and yet their success attracted the critics, who unanimously concurred in their exaltation of Glaspell and O'Neill. Glaspell's plays were performed in London in the 1920s to enthusiastic acclaim: she was ranked with Ibsen and Shaw, while Herbert Farjeon proclaimed her to be 'immeasurably superior to all American playwrights'.[7]

Few contemporary critics could resist the temptation to compare the output of the star Provincetowners, Glaspell and O'Neill: Isaac Goldberg suspected that the 'fundamental artistic difference' revealed by their plays 'may be rooted in the difference of sex as well as of temperament'. He went on to affirm that 'where O'Neill feels his thoughts, Glaspell thinks her feelings'.[8] Later commentators went further; Eugene Solow did not doubt that 'Susan Glaspell and Eugene O'Neill influenced each other in many more ways than one. Even to this day O'Neill has not forgotten his Glaspell.'[9] But O'Neill's biographers barely mention Susan Glaspell or her influence on the younger playwright: both she and George Cram Cook are granted at best a minor role in his artistic development.

Glaspell left the Provincetown Players once the original group had disbanded, returning to the theatre only to carry off the Pulitzer Prize in 1931 for her play *Alison's House*, while O'Neill, having experimented for all he was worth with the Provincetown audience, went on to write such classics as *Long Day's Journey into Night*.[10] O'Neill aspired to the Nobel Prize; Glaspell, to anonymity – the due reward for the difference Goldberg had pinpointed and which others also recognised: 'Her plays are different and curiously alive because her mind is unfettered by masculine predilection.'[11] In truth, Glaspell rebelled against all patriarchal codes which stifled the individual, but the plight of women inevitably interested her most of all.

Susan Glaspell was born in 1876 in Davenport, Iowa, into a traditional farming family whose values she challenged even in her earliest writing, protesting at imposed patterns of behaviour which suppressed the real self: 'Goodness knows we are cumbered and made uncomfortable enough by conventionality', she wrote in 1897, in a column entrusted to her by the *Davenport Weekly Outlook* when she was just twenty.[12]

The events of her own life pitted her against traditional Davenport society. After reading philosophy at Drake University, working on the *Des Moines Daily News*, and studying life in Chicago, the prodigal daughter returned to Davenport to become a full-time writer. She worked on her first full-length novel, *The Glory of the Conquered* (1909), and dutifully gave an annual lecture at the Tuesday Club (the local ladies' literary club), but she did not limit herself to such orthodox pursuits; she openly challenged her father's authority by 'declining to go to church in the morning and ostentatiously setting out for the Monist Society', which met on Sunday afternoons.[13] As if this were not enough to antagonise staid Davenporters, she fell in love with the founder of the Society, George Cram Cook, who would father two children and file two divorce suits before he got round to proposing marriage.

Glaspell and Cook were finally able to marry on 14 April 1913. They took refuge among the most radical and bohemian intellectuals of their times – the New York Greenwich Villagers. The Villagers were by no means a homogeneous group: although lawyers, teachers and writers by profession, they preferred Hutchins Hapgood's classification of their numbers: 'the Anarchists, the I.W.W.s, the extreme left wing of the Socialists, the females militantly revolutionary about sex-freedom, and the Cubists and Post-Impressionists in art'.[14] None of them was connected with the theatre, but they responded to the Dionysian call of the stage and dabbled incessantly in amateur theatricals at the Liberal Club and in the Boni brothers' bookshop. The latter venture developed into the Washington Square Players who in 1915 rejected a short play co-written by Susan Glaspell and her husband, *Suppressed Desires*, as being 'too special'.[15]

Like so many Greenwich Villagers, Cook and Glaspell were appalled by the box-office bias of Broadway: they fulminated against plays which followed a set pattern and left nothing whatsoever to the imagination. Intoxicated by the afflatus of the stage, they had applauded Maurice Browne's Little Theatre in Chicago and exulted at the Irish Players who had shown the courage to sweep aside conventions which threatened 'the humility of true feeling' (*RT*, p. 218); they itched for something similar in New York, refusing to fall sluggishly into that category of people who 'go to the theatre expecting to be bored' – as Gordon Craig dubbed most theatre audiences.[16] So, recognising the inherent histrionicism in the recent fad for psychoanalysis, they took to 'tossing lines back and forth at one another' (*RT*, p. 250) and together created *Suppressed Desires* – the play which, rejected by their peers, the Washington Square Players, was destined to ring up the curtain on the Provincetown Players, who eventually won fame in a converted stable on MacDougal Street, just off Washington Square.

The Greenwich Villagers worked their summers in Provincetown, on the very tip of Cape Cod: the sleepy fishing village offered them primitive clapboard cottages and minimal rents where they could escape from the steamy heat of New York – it had been discovered by Mabel Dodge, later famous for her liaison with D. H. Lawrence. As it happened, Hutchins Hapgood's wife Neith Boyce had dashed off a skit on the love affair between Dodge and Jack Reed (author of *Ten Days that Shook the World*) that had kept the Villagers speculating for a number of seasons. The Hapgoods offered their home for a joint performance of *Constancy* and *Suppressed Desires*.[17] Legend has it that Robert Edmond Jones (whom Dodge and others had sponsored during a year's study in Europe with Max Reinhardt, and who was later to become one of America's leading stage designers) improvised settings by 'making scenery from sofa cushions', and created a movable stage by asking the audience to face the ocean for the first play and then shuffle round towards the sitting room for the second.[18]

The performance was so successful that it was repeated: Cook cajoled Mary Heaton Vorse into cleaning out a rickety old fish-house on the end of her wharf, and the audience brought their own chairs. Cook was so enthralled by this histrionic experience that he bullied Vorse to allow the as-yet-unnamed Players to use the 'Wharf Theatre' throughout the following summer, 1916. He knocked up wooden benches, kicked friends into writing plays, and sold subscriptions for a theatre season – announcing a new play by Susan Glaspell as the chief attraction. Horrified, she protested that she did not know how to write plays: the answer was proof of Cook's faith in his wife's talent, and indicative of his vision of the theatre: 'Nonsense. You've got a stage, haven't you?' (*RT*, p. 255). Glaspell recounts in her biography of Cook, *The Road to the Temple* (1927), how 'the kitchen of a woman locked up in town' for the alleged murder of her husband – a true story she had covered when a reporter in Iowa – took shape as she sat on the bare boards of the Wharf, mulling over his injunction (*RT*, p. 256).

In *Trifles* (1916) Minnie Wright, who does not appear on stage, has been charged with strangling her husband; while the sheriff and his men search the house for clues to a motive, their wives gather a few items of clothing for the prisoner.[19] Mrs Peters and Mrs Hale are only nodding acquaintances, and the deferential, cowed sheriff's wife irritates the more defiant Mrs Hale, a robust farmer's wife, who will take no nonsense from woman or man. But, as they uncover hints of domestic unhappiness which unequivocally point to the motive the law needs in order to convict Minnie, an understanding grows between them until finally 'their eyes meet for an instant' sealing an unspoken bond (*T*, p. 44). They have found a strangled canary in Minnie Wright's sewing box, and fear that although the men have been unable to interpret the clues held by unsifted flour and dirty towels, they will not be blind to the analogy of the canary and the rope round Mr Wright's neck. Mrs Peters rushes forward to hide the evidence but is too agitated to touch the lifeless bird; Mrs Hale drops it deftly into her large coat pocket just before the men return to the kitchen.

The play focuses on the two women who tumble to the truth: they see the prison house that patriarchy has constructed of marriage. Although distressed by the murder, they can exonerate Minnie of her crime: looking round the kitchen they can identify with the burdens of her harsh existence and accept their responsibility for what happened: 'On, I *wish* I'd come over here once in a while! That was a crime! That was a crime! . . . We live close together and we live far apart. We all go through the same things – it's all just a different kind of the same thing' (*T*, p. 44). In *Trifles* Glaspell voiced her concern with the dilemmas of womanhood; she openly condoned the breaking of those patriarchal codes of behaviour which strangle women and deny them self-fulfilment.

She was to challenge patriarchy again and again in her plays, always intimating that suffering the punishment it meted out was preferable to stagnating within its laws. Outraged by the 1917 and 1918 Espionage and Sedition Acts she responded with *Inheritors*, which the Provincetown Players produced in 1920.[20] The setting is a Midwestern college campus which was founded by the idealist Silas Morton, one of the earliest settlers, and Felix Fejevary, an exiled Hungarian revolutionary, whose son is now on the Board of Trustees. The play opens in 1879 with a discussion of the pioneer days and of the importance of learning, and Act I ends with Morton's decision to bequeath his best land to the building of a college. Act II shows how the expansion of a college has brought about financial problems that must now be solved. Felix Fejevary Junior does his best to convince Senator Lewis that the state should appropriate the college and so assure its future. Lewis agrees but imposes one condition: Professor Holden, a radical idealist and supporter of conscientious objectors, must cease his subversive activities or go. By Act IV Fejevary has persuaded Holden of the advantages of silence, but he is then defeated by his niece – the grand-daughter of both Silas Morton and Felix Fejevary Sr – who insists on supporting Hindu students in their fight for Independence. As the play ends, Madeline Morton leaves for a court hearing; and there is no doubt that she will be sentenced to prison for her ideals.

This play is a feeling riposte to an historical moment, and although it is the least overtly feminist of Glaspell's plays the surface plot is merely a thin disguise for her disappointment with patriarchal society, with man's weakness and his readiness to forgo his ideals under pressure. Discreetly, Glaspell mocks a number of male myths, in particular the myth of male superiority. Just as in *Trifles* it is the supposedly ignorant women who uncover the clues to the murder, so here it is the 'inferior sex' as represented by Madeline which has the courage of self-sacrifice. Glaspell's 'leading' men, though generally endowed with redeeming virtues, are far from being supermen and frequently frustrate the expectations of the female protagonists.

In *Inheritors* she intelligently refuses to condemn or praise the individual outright, and her sympathies do waver between Holden

and Madeline, finally coming down on the side of the latter. Holden's
pusillanimous decision is excusable only in the light of his wife's
costly illness, while Madeline's action, though it will bring sorrow
on the family, is seen in the idealistic terms of the individual's self-
sacrifice in the cause of freedom. Glaspell was forever torn by the
dilemma facing women who wished to fulfil their potential but
were aware of the needs of their families. The young protagonist
of an early story, 'The Rules of the Institution', questions the valid-
ity of insisting on her freedom when this would hurt so many
loved ones: 'It seemed that affection and obligation were agents
holding one to one's place'; and yet Judith finally decides that 'she
owed no allegiance to an order that held life in chains'.[21] The novel
Fidelity (1915), in which Glaspell justifies her own principles of
behaviour, explores a young girl's 'right' to walk off with someone else's husband and the consequences of such an act. In both
cases Glaspell acknowledges the yearning of the individual for self-
expression, but is aware of the heartache it causes others.

In *The Verge* (1921), Glaspell examines the fate of the woman who
does not suppress her desires. The play was acclaimed by members
of the Heterodoxy – a radical women's club – with almost religious
respect: here was a playwright who dared to show how society
takes its revenge on a woman who had rebelled, and attained
herself.[22] Once again Glaspell portrays an intelligent woman caught
in the bonds of matrimony who commits murder to save her sanity.
Claire Archer, her protagonist, realises that the older order – symbolised by a plant she calls the 'Edge Vine' which grows in the
shape of a cross – has failed her: she can destroy the signifier, but
is helpless when faced with its signified. The new dispensation she
hopes for cannot, by its very nature, be articulated.

The play opens in a luscious and overheated greenhouse, representative of the socially restricted and shielded space Claire is forced
to inhabit; here she experiments with plants. She believes she can
exploit a technique of transplanting to create wholly new organisms
which are liberated from the previous forms and functions of plant
life. Tom, Dick and Harry (confidant, lover and husband) violate
her sanctum when they flee the symbolically cold house in search
of a more gratifying environment. Hoping to end their farcical
bickering, Claire attempts to express her Nietzschean desire to
overcome established patterns and to break through into whatever
lies beyond; of the three men in her life, only Tom gropes towards
an understanding of her disjointed utterances.

In Act II, Claire's sister Adelaide invades her study, a strangely twisted and uncannily lit tower, which is best interpreted as an outward sign of Claire's isolation and of her rejection of the world, though it is also a symbol of her disturbed mind. Claire is seen through 'a queer bulging window' (*V*, p. 78), about which Christine Dymkowksi has perceptively observed: 'It is most unusual for a playwright to separate characters from the audience with an actual physical barrier rather than a merely imagined fourth wall.'[23] Thus those entering this enclosed space can be construed not only as invaders of Claire's mind, but also as a schizophrenic splitting of her thought. Adelaide's mission is to convince her sister to play the part of the dutiful mother and wife, but Claire is too close to transcendence to take heed; now on the brink of uncovering her latest experiment, the plant she calls 'Breath of Life', she is overwhelmed by fear of retaliation from the God whose life-giving powers she has appropriated. Claire seeks a haven in the physical consummation of her relationship with the sympathetic Tom, but in deference to her superior spirit he denies her that ordinary human refuge, whereupon the second act ends with Claire's hysterical plea for 'Anything – everything – that will let me be nothing!' (*V*, p. 92).

The new plant which signals Claire's success in creating a hitherto unknown life-form is unveiled in the greenhouse in Act III. Yet the achievement is clearly ambivalent: any organism is condemned to repetition and stagnation unless it continually overcomes itself. Claire is fully conscious of that baleful dilemma; when Tom finally offers her his love she is appalled at the prospect of being engulfed by mediocrity and relentlessly chokes him to death. The murder mimics the suffocating norms of society which inevitably silence the creative urge in those who refuse to conform, but the family see Claire's convulsive action as final proof of her insanity. The play ends on a savagely ironic note as Claire chants the hymn 'Nearer, my God, to Thee' which Adelaide, intuiting blasphemy, had previously refused to sing in her presence. Claire, a female Faust, is now her own God and cannot be reached by societal structures and compunctions; she has broken out and is existentially free, alone in the transcendental beyond.

The Verge was Glaspell's most ambitious play and best exemplifies the degree to which the Provincetown Players had assimilated and made their own the innovative trends of European theatre. As C. W. E. Bigsby points out, 'few writers, before or since, ... attempted such a radical revisioning of all aspects of theatre'.[24] The play's tortured, highly symbolic setting, designed by Cleon Throckmorton, reminded its reviewers of the film *The Cabinet of Dr Caligari* (1919, released in the USA in the spring of 1921), and was welcomed as the first example of expressionism on the American stage.[25] Glaspell's treatment of her subject also goes beyond the critique of marriage to which Ibsen's *The Doll's House* and innumerable Broadway plays had, by 1921, inured the theatre-going public. Claire does not merely slam the door behind her; she encroaches on forbidden territory in her passion to create new life-forms. In a man, her Nietzschean over-reaching would be considered a normal function of aggression: in a woman, it amounts to the arrogation of faculties reserved for God – and for men. Claire has rejected the roles of wife, mother and mistress that are open to her, and rebels against the suppression of self that society would enforce upon a woman, only to discover that the penalty is total alienation. Paradoxically, in an age that considered hysteria to be the result of repression, she is repudiated as an hysteric by her family – and by most audiences, who have tended to see in her 'an almost clinical type for the psychoanalytical laboratory'.[26]

Claire may not appear as a conquering heroine – just as the protagonist of Glaspell's first novel, *The Glory of the Conquered* (1909), ostensibly fails in her self-imposed task. As *The Verge* ends we cannot doubt that Tennessee Williams's kind stranger is already at the door – yet the recognition of her insanity leaves room for a peculiar optimism since she has successfully abandoned the principles of this world for those of her own devising. Eugene O'Neill, writing of his own play *Diff'rent* (1920), perfectly caught the mood of *The Verge*:

There is a skin deep optimism and another higher optimism, not skin deep, which is usually confounded with pessimism. . . . The people who succeed and do not push on to a greater failure are the spiritual middle classers. . . . Only through the unattainable does man achieve a hope worth living and dying for – and so attain himself.[27]

Glaspell had taken care in *Inheritors* not to be too harsh on the male characters, but in *The Verge* she is not so generous; she allows each in turn to prove his inferiority to Claire. Tom, Dick and Harry, as their names suggest, are stereotypes; they are incapable of helping

Claire define herself fully in a patriarchal society or of protecting her from the consequences of transcending it. Harry, the husband, does his utmost to understand her, but his down-to-earth character is an impossible barrier to comprehension and communication. Dick paternally dismisses Claire's strange behaviour as 'the excess of a particularly rich temperament' (*V*, p. 65), whereas Tom commits the unforgivable error of offering her a bourgeois relationship.

The theme of male inferiority was always with Glaspell, as if its discovery surprised and pained her; as a result, her female protagonists have to be doubly courageous, but in Glaspell's eyes – paradoxically in ours – this does not lead to greater independence but accentuates the capacity for sacrifice and endurance characteristic of the woman of the nineteenth century. Glaspell was not alone in presenting woman as morally superior; indeed, such a protagonist was familiar to audiences of the 1910s and 1920s, who recognised in her superiority 'an index of feminine identity'.[28] The one satisfactory solution Glaspell can find to men's dependency – and to woman's desire for independence – is drastic. The protagonist of *Bernice* (1919) dies, and in death wields absolute power over her husband.[29] Neither the husband Craig nor her trusted friend Margaret who 'sees everything' (*B*, p. 10) arrive in time to hear Bernice's last words. The cause of death is never revealed; a long illness and a sudden, unexpected death are all we know. Bernice's marriage had not been successful; she was too independent to need Craig, an inferior writer whose work she could never admire, and he accordingly sought admiration from other women and was openly unfaithful to her. As in Claire's case, patriarchal society imposes on Bernice a two-fold denial of self-definition; as a woman in her own right she is trapped by marriage, and as a woman bound to her husband's love and professional unsuccess she is trapped by his inadequacy. Craig is a more dangerous opponent to Bernice than any of Claire's are to her; he wishes for the power to destroy and to reshape the terms of his existence but that is a faculty only Glaspell's female protagonists are given to exercise. Craig had presumably battled with Bernice for this power and had always lost; 'her life wasn't made by my life', he complains to Margaret (*B*, p. 17). In death, Bernice wins the battle once and for all. Before dying she extracts from Abbie, her servant, the promise to tell Craig that she had taken her own life. Through this ruse she hopes to confer on him the delusion of power over herself which he had always coveted, and indeed Craig convinces himself that he was 'everything to Bernice' (*B*, p. 19). On the other hand, Margaret cannot believe that her friend could have taken her own life and finally works out Bernice's Freudian logistics. Even from the grave, the female protagonist assumes power over the living, and as in the later plays the principal male character is shown to be undoubtedly weaker than his female counterpart.

Glaspell's men cannot understand their women; they are, without exception, vastly inferior intellectual and moral beings.[30] The logical corollary of this inequality would be that the women join forces against them, creating a higher caste; but Glaspell has no preconceived convictions of woman's superiority. Indeed, she can be equally as scathing of women's foibles as of men's: in *The Verge*, Claire's adolescent daughter, that 'creditable young American' who indiscriminately goes with 'all the girls' nauseates her, as does her sanctimonious sister, the prototypical self-sacrificing Mother (*V*, p. 74). Bernice and Margaret, whose bonding ensures the latter's final comprehension of her friend's action, have to contend with Craig's adoring sister who is prepared to defend him, come what may, while in *Inheritors* the pusillanimous Mrs Fejevary, in spite of her maternal feelings towards Madeline, can only echo her husband's arguments.

None the less, the possibility of real understanding between women attracted Glaspell, and her first play, *Trifles*, was in fact a study of female bonding – a central theme in the much later Pulitzer Prize-winning *Alison's House* (1930).[31] This thinly disguised study of Emily Dickinson begins after the protagonist's death, when we learn that Alison, the poet, had long since sacrificed her forbidden love in order to avoid bringing scandal on the family. Elsa, her niece, has run off with a married man, and even though that is precisely what Alison had *not* done, Elsa feels a special understanding between them. When a cache of unpublished poems by Alison is discovered, Elsa claims them for herself because she alone can 'know their value' (*AH*, p. 145). Alison, the seer, the one who always 'knew' and understood, and had the courage to sacrifice love and to find 'victory in defeat' – a constant Glaspellian motif – has left a legacy for all women in the form of her poetry (*AH*, p. 147).

Rebellion against the norms of society frequently takes the form of silence in Glaspell's plays and novels. The wronged woman in the novel *Fugitive's Return* (1929) loses the faculty of speech till she realises that, released from conventional ties, she is now free to regulate her life as she will. Similar self-denial of expression is the theme of the short story 'A Rose in the Sand' (1927) and of the play *The Outside* (1917). In these three pieces the protagonist perceives a new order – as in the miracle of a rose bush blossoming in the sand – and so finds her voice. In *Trifles, Inheritors* and *The Verge* the protagonist does nothing to impede her incarceration – or silencing – because she has already spoken out, she has 'grown beyond whatever we have words for': murder, political protest and the act of creation have freed her from convention and invested her with a divinity of her own.[32] Claire's triumph in particular has required the breaking of all established boundaries and her stumbling language reflects her struggle; she knows – as does Glaspell – that she is fighting for a freedom that has no name in the patriarchal idiom of society so it is not surprising that her articulacy almost succumbs to the inexpressible. Ludwig Lewisohn, a contemporary critic, attempted to explain Glaspell's uncertain diction: 'Miss Glaspell is morbidly frugal in expression, but nakedly candid in substance. . . . She is a dramatist, but a dramatist who is a little afraid of speech. Her dialogue is so spare that it often becomes arid.'[33] He then attributes this aridity to her Puritan background – whereas it is surely an attempt to surmount the constrictions of language, in particular as experienced by women.

The Provincetown Players survived only as long as George Cram Cook's vision of a communal theatre resisted the encroachments of professionalism. He had hoped to create a 'coral island of our own' on which he and his friends 'could have found the happiness of continuing ourselves toward perfection' while offering the American playwright a stage to experiment with (*RT*, p. 309). Dispirited by the lack of good native plays, and by the successful lure of the commercial theatre, he abandoned the venture in 1922, dragging his wife with him. John Corbin, reviewer for the *New York Times*, had earlier written that even if the Players had only produced Susan Glaspell, 'they would have justified their existence'.[34] She had perfected her artistry during those seven years, developing with the Players, and moving from realism to expressionism as she assimilated the techniques and devices of the modern drama. More importantly, she widened the thematic scope of the theatre; her work shows that women's concerns – trifles as some would say – are the stuff of drama. Women found themselves in Susan Glaspell's

words; they apprehended the inner springs of their being as her
protagonists re-enacted the sacred drama of their history.

NOTES

1. June Schlueter (ed.), *American Drama: The Female Canon* (London and
    Toronto: Associated University Presses, 1990); Enoch Brater (ed.),
    Feminine Focus: The New Women Playwrights (New York: Oxford
    University Press, 1989).
2. William Butler Yeats, 'Three Songs to the Same Tune', in *King of the
    Great Clock Tower* (Dublin: Cuala Press, 1934) pp. 36–8.
3. Susan Glaspell, *The Road to the Temple* (New York: Frederick A. Stokes,
    1927) p. 249. Future references will be included in the text and
    abbreviated to *RT*.
4. Kenneth MacGowan, *Footlights Across America* (New York: Harcourt
    Brace, 1929) p. 48.
5. Copeau's comment is quoted in Norman H. Paul, 'Jacques Copeau
    Looks at the American Stage, 1917–1919', *Educational Theatre Journal*
    (March 1977) p. 61. The Provincetown Players' announcement (in the
    Provincetown Scrapbook, Beinecke Library, Yale) for the season 1922–
    3 states their aims during the seven years of their existence.
6. William Archer, in his review of *The Emperor Jones* for the *Evening Post*,
    had attributed to the sand dunes of Cape Cod the honour of being
    'the real birthplace of the New American Drama'. His words were
    jubilantly quoted by the Players in their announcement for the 1921–
    2 season (Provincetown Scrapbook, Beinecke Library, Yale).
7. Herbert Farjeon, 'Odds and Ends', *Westminster Weekly*, 7 February
    1926. See also J. K. Prothero, 'The Drama: Over the Top', *G.K.'s Weekly*,
    11 April 1925.
8. Isaac Goldberg, *The Drama of Transition: Native and Exotic Playcraft*
    (Cincinnati, Ohio: Stewart Kidd, 1922) pp. 472–3.
9. Eugene Solow, 'American's Great Woman Dramatist: Susan Glaspell',
    The World, 9 February 1930. Solow goes on to say: 'and I think a
    comparison of Nina and Sam, Ned and Charlie in *Strange Interlude*
    with Claire Archer and her Tom, Dick and Harry combination in *The
    Verge* will bear me out'. For more on the influence of Glaspell on
    O'Neill, see Linda Ben-Zvi, 'Susan Glaspell and Eugene O'Neill', *The
    O'Neill Newsletter*, vol. 6, no. 2 (1982) pp. 21–9, and 'Susan Glaspell
    and Eugene O'Neill: the Imagery of Gender', *Eugene O'Neill News-
    letter*, vol, 10, no. 1 (1986) pp. 22–7.
10. According to Edna Kenton, the unofficial historian of the Province-
    town Players, O'Neill subjected his audiences to incomprehensible
    theatrical devices to test their endurance. He 'played' with them, in
    order to build his later plays on their 'stark laboratory reactions
    to his own experimentations' (quoted in Edna Kenton, 'Province-

town and MacDougal Street', in George Cram Cook, *Greek Coins* (New York: George H. Doran, 1925) p. 24).

11. This quotation from the *Illustrated London News* is taken from an undated and unsigned clipping in the Susan Glaspell papers in the Berg Collection, New York Public Library.

12. Susan Glaspell, 'Social Life', *Weekly Outlook*, vol. 2, no. 11 (13 March 1897) p. 7. This was an unsigned column that appeared regularly in the *Weekly Outlook*; Glaspell was Society Editor for the paper from its first issue, 11 July 1896, until she left Davenport for Drake University, Des Moines, to study for a degree in philosophy in September 1897. In a monograph, *Susan Glaspell: Voice from the Heartland* (Macomb, Ill.: Western Illinois University, 1983), Marcia Noe argues convincingly that the 'Social Life' columns were written by Glaspell.

13. The Monist Society was founded by George Cram Cook and Floyd Dell as a gesture of rebellion against the Davenport Socialist Party, which, as Glaspell wrote, 'had to be treated a little too respectfully' (*RT*, p. 191).

14. Hutchins Hapgood, *A Victorian in the Modern World* (1939; Seattle and London: University of Washington Press, 1972) p. 379.

15. Edna Kenton, 'The Provincetown Players and the Playwrights' Theatre', copy of unpublished manuscript, Beinecke Library, Yale, p. 5.

16. Edward Gordon Craig, 'The Art of the Theatre: the First Dialogue' (1905), in J. Michael Walton, *Craig on Theatre* (London: Methuen, 1983) p. 55.

17. Susan Glaspell and George Cram Cook, *Suppressed Desires*, in Margaret Gardner Mayorga (ed.), *Representative One-Act Plays by American Authors* (Boston, Mass.: Little, Brown, 1922).

18. Helen Deutsch and Stella Hanau, *The Provincetown: A Story of the Theatre* (New York: Farrar & Rinehart, 1931) p. 6.

19. Susan Glaspell, *Trifles*, in C. W. E. Bigsby (ed.), *Plays by Susan Glaspell* (Cambridge: Cambridge University Press, 1987). Future references will be included in the text, abbreviated to *T*.

20. Susan Glaspell, *Inheritors*, in ibid.

21. Susan Glaspell, 'The Rules of the Institution', *Harper's Monthly*, vol. 128 (January 1914) p. 208.

22. Susan Glaspell, *The Verge*, in Bigsby, *Plays by Susan Glaspell*. Future references will be included in the text, abbreviated to *V*. For the Heterodites' reaction to *The Verge*, see Hapgood, *A Victorian in the Modern World*, p. 377.

23. Christine Dymkowski, 'On the Edge: the Plays of Susan Glaspell', *Modern Drama*, vol. 33, no. 1 (March 1988) p. 101.

24. Bigsby, *Plays by Susan Glaspell*, p. 19.

25. Kenneth MacGowan acknowledged that Throckmorton's set was 'expressionistic'; he first used the term with reference to a whole play apropos Eugene O'Neill's *The Hairy Ape* (1922). See Kenneth MacGowan, 'The New Play', *New York Evening Globe*, 15 November 1921; and Mardi Valgemae, *Accelerated Grimace: Expressionism in the*

American Drama of the 1920s (Carbondale, Ill.: Southern Illinois Press, 1972) p. 179.

26.   Goldberg, *The Drama of Transition*, p. 475.

27.   Eugene O'Neill, 'Damn the Optimists!', quoted in the *New York Tribune*, 13 February 1921, and in Oscar Cargill, *Eugene O'Neill and His Plays* (London: Peter Owen, 1962) p. 104. Although O'Neill never saw *The Verge* he may well have read *The Glory of the Conquered*, and since he shared Glaspell's enthusiasm for Nietzsche's doctrine of self-perfection it is not surprising to find words that describe her feelings in his writing.

28.   Judith L. Stevens, 'Gender Ideology and Dramatic Convention in Progressive Era Plays, 1890–1920', in *Theatre Journal*, vol. 41 (1989) p. 54.

29.   Susan Glaspell, *Bernice* (London: Ernest Benn, 1924). Future references will be included in the text, abbreviated to *B*.

30.   Isaac Goldberg, comparing the plays of Eugene O'Neill and Susan Glaspell, observes: 'O'Neill's women do not understand their menfolk; Glaspell's men do not understand their women.' In Glaspell's case, Goldberg attributes this lack of understanding to the fact that the men are 'eminently normal' (*The Drama of Transition*, p. 477).

31.   Susan Glaspell, *Alison's House* (New York: Samuel French, 1930). Future references will be included in the text, abbreviated to *AH*.

32.   Friedrich Nietzsche, *The Twilight of the Idols* (1889), trans. R. J. Hollingdale (Harmondsworth, Middx: Penguin, 1986) p. 83.

33.   Ludwig Lewisohn, *The Drama and the Stage* (New York: Harcourt, Brace, 1922) p. 103.

34.   John Corbin, 'Seraphim and Cats', *New York Times*, 30 March 1919, sec. 8, p. 2.

2
Eugene O'Neill
ERIC MOTTRAM

For the performance on 28 July 1916, the Provincetown Players in Massachusetts chose for their Wharf Theatre a one-act play by Eugene O'Neill. This play, *Bound East for Cardiff*, displayed materials to which the 28-year-old writer would return, and develop, for the rest of his life. The forecastle of the tramp steamer *Glencairn* is a tight enclosure, the home of the lower-deck seamen – lower-class or unclassed, de-nationed men existing in a floating, mobile pseudo-home among basic objects: bunks, a lamp, oilskins, seaboots. Movement in enclosure during a voyage or journey, but a stasis of lives – in fact, a sense of enclosure that edges into a trap.

The tramp moves across the ocean in fog – moves forward as the dying seaman, Yank, goes back into his memories, and brings them forward. His monologue, in seaman's language, dominates the brief action. His life memories recall an enclosed sailor's existence of hard work, poor pay, a succession of ports, drunken fights, an unattached life: as he says, in an early O'Neill entrance into a dimension beyond day-to-day existence, 'without no one to care whether you're alive or dead'. Then his guilt surfaces: he admits to killing a man in drunken self-defence. He fears judgement in an after-life. Driscoll, the man he confides in, tries to help: 'Let your conscience be aisy'; but it is too late. Yank is 'bound' to his past and his death, as the ship is 'bound' for Cardiff.[1]

Yank also reveals he wanted an alternative life – deeply characteristic of O'Neill – a farm home, an enclosure inland (agrarian), another kind of binding to the natural, but one which he believes would have ensured security. So his monologue unmasks a character in crisis, a process O'Neill will continually produce in his theatre – a sense of a life as space-time layers of strategies for survival in a hostile world.

By 1924, the farm home in *Desire under the Elms* is conceived far from dreams of work and family security. The O'Neill vision already contradicts that part of the American 1920s which existed

21

in post-war Boom euphoria, and is nearer to the threatened urban American survivals in Scott Fitzgerald's novels of the 1920s – the conclusion of *This Side of Paradise* in 1920 and the whole structure of *The Great Gatsby* in 1925, the disillusioned mobility in Dos Passos's *Manhattan Transfer*, also in 1925, and the sense of entrapment and punishment in Hemingway's *A Farewell to Arms* in 1929.

O'Neill had read Conrad and Jack London, whose works augmented his own 16 months of seamanship, and had absorbed these novelists' awareness of non-human forces controlling human survival. In 1907 O'Neill attended ten consecutive performances of Ibsen's *Hedda Gabler* on New York's Broadway, and in 1911 attended all the New York productions of Yeats and Synge performed by the Abbey Theatre of Dublin. He had read Strindberg, and for the Provincetown Players' production of *The Ghost Sonata*, on 3 January 1924, wrote a programme note, quoting a passage from him. It offers O'Neill's position as much as the Swedish playwright's:

> People talk of the Joy of Life as if it consists in dancing and farcical idiocy. For me, the Joy of Life consist in the mighty and terrible struggles of existence, in the capability of experiencing something, of learning something.[2]

At this time composing *Desire under the Elms*, O'Neill wrote:

> Strindberg was the precursor of all modernity in our present theatre . . . the modern of moderns, the greatest interpreter in the theatre of the characteristic spiritual conflicts which constitute the drama – the blood! – of our lives today. He carried naturalism to a logical attainment of such poignant intensity that . . . we must classify a play like *The Dance of Death* as 'super-naturalism'.[3]

O'Neill believed that a form of 'super-naturalism' was needed to 'comprehend intuitively . . . that self-defeating life'. The old 'naturalism' or 'realism', once daring as 'snapshots of each other in every graceless position', and 'the banality of surface', must end. We must move on to

> some as yet unrealized region where our souls, maddened by loneliness and the ignoble inarticulateness of flesh, are slowly evolving their new language of kinship.

Strindberg knew and suffered with our struggle years before many of us were born. He expressed it by intensifying the method of his time and by foreshadowing both in content and form the methods to come . . . all that is enduring in what we loosely call 'Expressionism' – all that is artistically valid and sound theatre.[4]

O'Neill coins a term for these techniques: Strindberg's 'behind-life'. It is deeply related to Henry James's 'the thing hideously behind' (see *The Golden Bowl*, 1904).

Strindberg's *The Father*, *Creditors* and *The Dance of Death* emerge from a Darwinian survivalism – and this they have in common with the plots of Jack London, Theodore Dreiser, Frank Norris and other American Naturalists of the early twentieth century: a struggle for existence that all life has in common, a sense of the necessarily sacrificial within the social and human. In Ibsen's plays it takes the forms of dominant inheritance – psychological, pathological and social. Characters either resist and yield, or resist and are radically changed. O'Neill once said that Nietzsche's *The Birth of Tragedy* was 'the most stimulating book on drama ever written', and he quoted from it in the programme for *The Great God Brown* in 1926. The Dionysian factor in tragedy is not only placed in the character of Dion Anthony, but in the beliefs of Cybel at the end of this play: 'always love and conception and birth and pain again – spring bearing the intolerable chalice of life again!'

In 1928, *Lazarus Laughed* uses ideas in *Thus Spake Zarathustra* concerning the future of faith in a resurrected Man of Power after the apparent death of God – a Nietzsche phrase which Edmund Tyrone quotes in *Long Day's Journey into Night* in 1941. And the living-room bookcase in that play contains, O'Neill's instructions to the director and reader state, works by Zola, Ibsen, Shaw and Nietzsche. In his 1936 Nobel Prize speech, O'Neill said that his debt to Strindberg stayed profound: 'For me, he remains as Nietzsche remains in his sphere, the Master'.

So O'Neill's plays were composed out of a necessary reading of dominant literature for his time, and he strenuously placed the dynamics of theatre in the interactions between large forces of nature and religion, between the local forces of human responsibility and broader forces of human psychological inevitabilities. *Long Day's Journey* closes down in a sense of continuity of these conditions. The characters have learned the conditions of monologue and dialogue in the house enclosure and from the enclosures of their

lives. Now they continue. The play joins the company of Chekhov's
Three Sisters and *Uncle Vanya,* and of Sartre's *Huis Clos,* with its
ultimate line of enclosure and continuity: *'Eh bien, continuons.'*

The three sea-and-ship *Glencairn* plays of 1916 are already naturalist and determinist, playing into enclosure within an elegiac mood
– a mood exemplified in *The Moon of the Caribees* (1918) by 'a
melancholy negro chant' and 'the full moon' that enclose the ship.
O'Neill describes it as 'the mood of moonlight made audible'. Inside it, the seaman Olson saves his pay to return to his family farm
in Sweden, a dream maliciously destroyed by robbers who drug
him and place him on a rotting ship voyaging round Cape Horn to
Liverpool, bound West on a long voyage which will never end in
a farm home. Olson is an initial type in O'Neill's overwhelming
sense of limited movement and curtailed freedom. As these assumptions entered the Depression years of the 1930s, and the collapse
of American capitalism, O'Neill's plays, like Hemingway's fictions,
were contrasted with the rebellious, analytical optimism – the
possibility of future change – in American 'writers on the Left', to
use the title of Daniel Aaron's classic study, including major poets
like Muriel Rukeyser, George Oppen and Louis Zukofsky. Hart
Crane and Ezra Pound maintained the future-looking Right, and
Yeats, Eliot and Hemingway shared allegiances to Spenglerian,
Christian or occult repetitive cycles of what Joyce, in *Finnegans Wake,*
encapsulated as 'the seim anew'.

In the 1930s, off-Broadway theatre's politically active groups
were formed to challenge this kind of deadlock – in particular the
Group Theatre, whose initial major political and Left dramatist was
Clifford Odets. O'Neill's work in the 1930s and 1940s did not directly
engage such politics of criticism and the desire for revolutionary
change. He finished the first draft of *Mourning Becomes Electra* in
February 1930, three months after the stock market crashed. His
victims were not the hungry, unemployed, sick, starved and suicidal
Americans of this decade.

Back in 1916, the seaman Olson becomes an unthinking victim of
vicious manipulation. In *Beyond the Horizon* in 1918, at the end of
the First World War, O'Neill produces Robert and Andrew Mayo
caught in dreams of owning farms and trapped in a long voyage
from home which proves disastrous. O'Neill circles in the sphere of
Edgar Allan Poe, in fictions of enclosure, burial, masks and the sea
as an arena of reversals. Like Poe, he became a popular author.
From *The Emperor Jones* in 1921 onwards, his plays were usually

successful in New York. They contained no esoteric literary or avant-garde risks – beyond clear and direct uses of expressionism. His themes were as central to common American belief structures as those of his contemporary John Steinbeck, and the films made of them. When James Tyrone criticises his sons for their 'Socialist babble', he is very much part of popular reactionary belief and part of O'Neill.

The rhythmic accumulations from the past which augment and enter present lives (from the 1916 plays through to *Long Day's Journey into Night*) are irresistible, operating as small rafts for limited but rescued life, as they do in Chekhov's plays. The Tyrone family reiterates the same language of sounds, gestures and words until an audience is saturated with an overwhelming echo system, visually and orally. The action has little or nothing of, for instance, Céline's 1932 satirical perceptions of America and the human condition, *Journey to the End of the Night*. The Tyrone play inherits, as the family in *Mourning Becomes Electra* inherits in 1929 to 1931, and these inheritances cannot move towards comedy – that is, the comforts of restoration of some previous status quo, signalled in the usual conventions of hopeful marriages. The Mannon family is tracked down before, in and after the family mansion. The home means the building as enclosure of dynasty and destiny. The triple basis of O'Neill's tightest bonds against the new are the triple models of Civil War which brings no relief or renewal, the classic ancient Greek tragic trilogy, the *Oresteia* of Aeschylus, and Freud's early twentieth-century psychoanalytical plot, derived from the myth of the primal horde and the ancient Greek tragedy of Sophocles' *Oedipus the King*. O'Neill's determinism is paradoxically a security system rather than an early-warning system. For the old systems of 'gods' and their controls he now inserts the assumed inevitabilities of war, classical tragedy and classical psychology. In his 'Working Notes and Extracts from a Fragmentary Work Diary', first published in the *New York Herald-Tribune* on 3 November 1931, O'Neill wrote:

Modern psychological drama using one of the old legend plots of Greek tragedy for its basic theme. . . . Is it possible to get modern psychological approximation of [a] Greek sense of fate into such a play, which an intelligent audience of today, possessed of no belief in gods or supernatural retribution, could accept and be moved by?[5]

In practice, he altered the Aeschylan pattern. In the 'Working Notes' he is explicit: he will work at the figure of Electra as the god-punished example of 'tragic fate', while retaining his concept of 'a modern psychological drama'. As Lavinia Mannon, his Electra, faces her Ibsen ghosts from a corrupt past, and finally enters the House of Mannon as the curtain falls, there is no possibility of a future society of difference. In Aeschylus, the Furies who torment, with guilt for matricide, become Eumenides, forces of absolution and fertility. After Orestes' trial for matricide, the gods of judgement – Apollo and Aphrodite – decide for balance, reason, restoration – passion and darkness are turned towards rationality and light. However, at the end of O'Neill's play, Orin's death is an agony and Lavinia ends in sterile inheritance. The mood is twilight and moonlight, darkness and candle-light. The action opens with 'black bars of shadow' cast from the columns of the Greek-style portico of the mansion – so that the walls become a cage, an enclosure resistant to change. In Act III of Part ii, 'The Hunted', the corpse of Ezra Mannon, returned from the Civil War, is actually on the stage. When the action shifts to Adam Brant, the Aegisthus figure, at the stern of his ship an old seaman sings the sad sea-shanty 'Shenandoah', and talks about the good old days which will not return, and the assassination of Abraham Lincoln. When Orin murders Brant – on stage – and Brant resembles Ezra Mannon, Orin says: 'I've killed before – over and over.' The 'Working Notes' are explicit that the sea-shanty is 'a sort of theme song – its simple sad rhythm of hopeless sea longing peculiarly significant'.

Writing on a production of the *Oresteia* in 1965, Barthes historicises the action:

> The *Oresteia* tells us what the men of its period sought to transcend, the obscurantism they tried to clarify; but it tells us at the same time that these efforts are an anachronism for us, that the new gods it sought to establish are gods we conquered in our turn.[6]

But O'Neill is obsessed with what controls destinies, and this is why classical tragedy appealed. But to de-historicise the Greek into the eternal, twentieth-century concepts of control have to be utilised as replacements, in order to leave the past, the ghosts, the gods and the conflicts intact. O'Neill's characters have to live mythically – just as Freud's Oedipal control pattern is mythical. The play is dramatically forceful, grand theatre – a highly professional display of skills at the command of beliefs that are determinedly presented. Aeschylean Greece, America, and Freud's Vienna are layered masks, or superimposed sites.

O'Neill's naturalism was and is deeply constituted in American popular economic and existential belief – a programme of forces to which major writers and their audiences adhered and adhere, and in which is found such coherences as they require. The allegiance extends from Stephen Crane and Dreiser through Hemingway to O'Neill. Lavinia finally turns away from her lover saying: 'Love isn't permitted to me. The dead are too strong.' She enters the family home or mausoleum alone, to live shut up with ancestral determinism, Oedipal pressures, the inability to break with natural forces – a pattern which, as in William Faulkner's fiction, is given as a curse. When Lavinia says: 'I know they will see to it I live a long time! It takes the Mannons to punish themselves for being born!', It is like a replay of *Oedipus at Colonnus* for Americans. W. B. Yeats translated the key passage in Sophocles:

> Never to have lived is best, ancient writers say;
> Never to have drawn breath of life, never to
> have looked into the eye of day . . . [7]

The strong American line included Jack London, intellectually reared on Darwin and Marx, who admitted his belief to a friend in 1899: 'The different families of man must yield to law – LAW, inexorable, blind, unreasoning law, which has no knowledge of good or ill, right or wrong.'[8] In *The Iceman Cometh* in 1939 Larry Slade will voice his beliefs in the tradition: 'Life is too much for me! I'll be a weak fool looking with pity at the two sides of everything till the day I die! May that day come soon!'

Law is the father, the thing before, the inheritance compulsion, the inescapable, the inevitable, the desire for law itself, the Darwinian irrefutable forces. To produce a comedy within such law O'Neill turned from *Mourning Becomes Electra* to *Ah, Wilderness* in 1932 – Tennessee Williams would have similar consequent problems with *Period of Adjustment* in 1960. Williams's title suggests the issues: comedy is traditionally adjustment, a return to stability, often with an intervention of stoicism, but rarely from revolutionary change. O'Neill called his play 'a comedy of recollection', and it is therefore an action parallel to the family recollections and repetitions in *Long*

Day's Journey into Night, seven years later. The seventeen-year-old Richard Miller revolts against the parental and the capitalist systems. He gets drunk, reads proscribed books, and has sex with a prostitute, thinks of himself as the Dionysian artist Lovborg in *Hedda Gabler*. The tone is gentle, and only gently satirical. Richard and his girl Essie find love, and it is a prelude to finding a continuity of life in the parental world. Where Lavinia entered the family house as a determinist prison, Richard and Essie kiss and – in O'Neill's directions – 'they move quietly out of the moonlight, back into the darkness of the front parlour'.

This dark room is not Lavinia's darkness, nor the dark room in which Mary Tyrone will live, after *Long's Day's Journey into Night*, in her drugged condition. O'Neill's tone is compassionate, gently ironical, gently sad, tender about the necessities of a determined life. It was O'Neill's most popular play. No one is masked; the young couple re-enter the social scene without terror. The date is 1906; the date of production is during the Depression.

In *Strange Interlude* (1927), a middle-class American woman adjusts to a lifetime of adjustment, and the audience knows more about the psychology of the processes than the cast. O'Neill concentrates on his 'drama of souls' in conflict by using that sense of duplicity, of a life behind the social surface, which psychoanalysis had produced in popular estimates of human behaviour. By 1927, translations of Freud had enabled a selection of his psychology to enter the popular American typography of life. The audience is given the interior life in a series of monologues – they are not asides or soliloquies – which only they can hear. The reader of the text has also a detailed account of the concealed and revealed positions. Once again, O'Neill's drama moves towards the novel, and in this case towards those 'stream of consciousness' fictions made fashionable after Joyce's *Ulysses* in 1922, and neatly parodied by Groucho Marx a few years later, following the popularity of O'Neill's play. (In one of his 1930s films, Groucho Marx turns to the audience, prior to a seduction scene with Margaret Dumont, and says: 'Pardon me while I have a strange interlude'.) The presentation of the hidden, the secret, the taboo is popular – a resistance to censorship. The play's 426 performances made it O'Neill's longest run, and produced his third Pulitzer Prize. An intermittent flow of interiority might sound ludicrous. In practice, it is not – as is proved by an excellent television production in which the private statements were given a separate sound-track, and by the 1984 London production with Glenda Jackson as Nina Leeds. The form is necessary for the audience to experience the tensions between interior and exterior life, and the trauma it causes in the heroine. Her father had prevented her marriage to her lover, an aviator. After he is killed in the First World War she feels guilty, becomes a nurse in a military hospital, and has many affairs with wounded, convalescent men. Her self-punishment does not relieve the guilt; but once her father dies, she marries a decent, ordinary man she does not love but who will give her a child. Then she discovers there is insanity in his family . . . and so on: a full panoply of the sexual problematic and its analysis, just short of what we have today as 'soap' serials in television. The action takes at least five hours to perform.

The theatre problem is clear: *analysed* emotions are diminished in emotional force for an audience; the action remains determinist and utterly explicit, as Nina Leeds makes clear at one point:

> the only living life is in the past and future . . . the present is an interlude . . . strange interlude in which we call on past and future to bear witness we are living.

Strange Interlude exemplifies a main pitch of resolution in O'Neill's theatre: a play of stoic adjustment. In his next play, *Dynamo* (1928), he returned to major complex themes of science, sexuality and religion. In a letter to the theatre critic George Jean Nathan he gave his aim:

> [to] dig at the roots of the sickness of Today as I feel it – the death of the old God and the failure of Science and Materialism to give any Satisfying new One for the surviving primitive religious instinct to find a meaning for life in, and to comfort its fears of death. It seems to me anyone trying to do big work nowadays must have this big subject behind all the little subjects of his plays and novels, or he is simply scribbling around on the surface of things and has no more real status than a parlour entertainer.[9]

As Ingmar Bergman once stated: 'All drama that is not about man's relationship to God is nonsense.' But for 'God' we have to read: any dominant external force or demonic inevitability, before and within which human life is under scarcely tolerable control. Or is believed to be. Americans inherit Ralph Waldo Emerson's question: 'How shall a man escape from his ancestors, or draw off from his veins the black drop which he drew from his father's or his mother's life?' Passed through Nietzsche's death of God, and what Freud ironically called 'the family romance', the question becomes O'Neill's theatre – and it is never dominated by one member of a family's point of view. That is the strength of *Long Day's Journey into Night*. Mary Tyrone believes 'I was healthy before Edmund was born. But bearing Edmund was the last straw.' The sibling tension between Edmund and his elder brother Jamie emerges precisely here – the older son's hatred of his younger brother for causing the mother's condition, the cause of his own alcoholism. The action circulates beliefs and causal excuses, and is never solutionary but stoic and, in O'Neill's words, written with 'deep pity and understanding and forgiveness'. The action interweaves love and hostility, compassion and bitter resentment, accusation and apology. At the final curtain, the audience is cut off from what will continue possibly for ever – it has sufficient energy. But there can be no change in what are assumed to universals – or what O'Neill's Greeks called fate.

Until 1924 O'Neill's plays concerned unthinking and apparently dominated characters – homeless figures who cannot articulate their alienations. Most of them are male and proletarian. There followed plays showing sensitive women and men, at least partly intellectual, conscious and articulate, whose actions expose something of the complexities of living. But they remain controlled under erotic and family forces that reduce them to exhaustion, death, drugs, stoic abandonment of choice. The political and economic system is shown as an immediate programme of further determining forces, apprehended as order, and therefore – ambiguously – both as security and a cause for resistance.

In *The Iceman Cometh* (1939) the men who doss in Harry Hope's saloon live beyond lost careers and wasted abilities, dreams of alcoholic self-salvation – what O'Neill calls 'pipe-dreams', a kind of haze of drugged minimal survival. They constitute a kind of male family, with outriding women. But they do survive and their talk is highly alert. Larry Slade, the only analytical outsider, has a face-mask which expresses the 'tired tolerance' of 'a pitying but weary old priest'. The saloon is indeed a religious scene of derelicts in a ritual. It requires virtuoso acting alertness to sustain O'Neill's long action. Its myth is: illusion sustains life – even if it means lying to oneself – and belief in a change of circumstances in some ever-elusive tomorrow. Hickey forces the men to another kind of 'truth', and through confronting the conditions of his own life, the murder of his wife, he disrupts the family of Hope. It is only reunited with the restoration of illusion – a play of readjustment, and virtually without cynicism. It questions analysis, the classic proposition: Know thyself. Hickey, the Great Salesman, for whom the derelicts wait annually, unfreezes them, once a year. A false spring god in the mask of death confronts the masks of peace.

He is paralleled by the suicide of Don Parritt, a young man who betrayed an anarchist organisation to the police, thereby causing his mother's life imprisonment. Parritt's self-punishment, Hickey's murder of a wife he pretended to love, Slade's truthful death in life without illusions – this triple information surfaces in the Hope saloon. In 1939, after the rise of Stalin and Hitler, the Spanish Civil War and the apparent collapse of American capitalism, just as the world was about to enter another global conflict, O'Neill has Slade, an ex-Syndicalist-Anarchist, say:

> To hell with the truth! As the history of the world proves, the truth has no bearing on anything. It's irrelevant and immaterial, as the lawyers say . . .
> The tomorrow movement is a sad and beautiful thing too!

O'Neill is voicing a common, even popular, estimate of the times. Slade ends up exhausted – an example of what Fitzgerald called in 1936 the failure of 'the ability to function'. He is seated in 'the grandstand of philosophical detachment'. At a press conference, answering questions on his play, in 1946, O'Neill said:

> the war has thrown me completely off base. . . . There is a feeling around, or I'm mistaken, of fate. Kismet, the negative fate; not in the Greek sense. . . . A sort of unfair *non sequitur*, as though events, as though life, were being manipulated just to confuse us . . . a big kind of comedy that doesn't stay funny very long. I've made some use of it in *The Iceman*.[10]

But in a letter to Lawrence Langer, O'Neill also said:

> there are moments in [*The Iceman Cometh*] that suddenly strip the soul of a man stark naked, not in cruelty or moral superiority, but with an understanding compassion which sees him as a victim of

the ironies of life and of himself. These moments are for me the
depth of tragedy, with nothing more that can be possibly said.[11]

Once again, it is the presence of unmasking that concerns O'Neill
– the theatre ritual of revelation of the inevitable, the 'behind life',
the inheritance. Theatre for him was *the* social medium in which he
could present rather than analyse and solve – could in fact always
dramatise his 1922 belief:

> our emotions are a better guide than our thoughts. Our emotions
> are instinctive. They are the result not only of our individual
> experiences but of the experiences of the whole human race, back
> through the ages.[12]

While not, of course, restricted to American belief, this is a peculiarly American identification of the self with universals. It is effective
in writers as apparently different as Melville, Whitman, Faulkner
and Arthur Miller: the desire to write as a laureate of popular belief
identifying self with universal and therefore permissive behaviour
– a risk at any time, but critical when transferred to national conduct. O'Neill's needs for covering beliefs, security constants, bases
to justify stoic response to a decaying world – the undoubted world
of his 1916 to 1953 career – had also stern personal bases. Once that
is known, his work becomes an act of extraordinarily courageous
creativity. It is persuasively described by Mary Heaton Vorse in
Time and the Town: A Provincetown Chronicle. As a founding member
of the Provincetown Players, who performed O'Neill's first play,
Bound East for Cardiff, her contact with the young dramatist is
particularly valuable:

> this recluse who shunned people was afraid to be alone. The
> unfriendly universe pressed down upon him in the dark and
> filled him with the foreboding of naked primitive man . . . fear of
> the unknown, fear of the dark and the universe . . . No one has
> written a story of his life or his unending struggle with an empty
> universe . . . The surrounding mystery and terror of life were
> always with him.[13]

Young Americans in the 1920s and 1930s got an education in
the theatre, for almost every subject of importance was discussed

in the best plays of these years, from social and political philosophy to sexual morality. The censors, official and unofficial, had not yet moved in.[14]

Writing in 1960, Willard Thorp is properly estimating theatre vitality in that decade. In New York the American playwrights included Lillian Hellman, Robert Sherwood, Sidney Howard, Maxwell Anderson and Eugene O'Neill. Europeans produced included Ibsen, Strindberg, J. M. Synge, Ferenc Molnar, Pirandello and Shaw. At Harvard University, George Pierce Baker's theatre centre, *47 Workshop*, thrived, and the courses included the apparatus and techniques of theatre: lighting, cycloramas, acting and direction. O'Neill arrived there at a time when he was absorbed in Strindberg's *The Dance of Death* and Dostoyevsky's *The Idiot*. He had already attended performances of Ibsen, Yeats, Synge and other masters in New York. The Moscow Art Theatre appeared in that city in 1922 and 1923. In Boston, Chicago, Cleveland, Baltimore, Dallas and other major cities, serious theatre groups were established – in fact, it is estimated that there were at least 500. In New York, the Washington Square Players – founded in 1915 – performed Chekhov, Ibsen and Maeterlinck as well as local Americans authors. Veterans of the group founded the Theatre Guild in 1918, which became the most influential company in American theatre Guild in 1918, which became the most influential company in American theatre history – they were to perform O'Neill's *Marco's Millions* in 1928. O'Neill's own Provincetown Players were founded in Massachusetts in 1915, and worked in New York until the Depression of 1929. Particularly significant for O'Neill, the European expressionist theatre became a major theatre foundation: 'By 1924 any little theatre in America which knew its business had produced [Georg] Kaiser's *From Morn to Midnight* or [Ernst] Toller's *Man and the Masses*.'[15] These were plays of maximum social analysis and criticism, using maximum sound and visual devices of theatre – a theatre of ideas employing experimental forms, internationally available from Moscow to Dallas.

O'Neill became a foremost experimenter in theatre and the major presenter of the schizophrenia of living in a highly competitive society. Search for identity, a guiding faith, some release from social restriction, some emergence of repressed desire without disaster, characterised the 1920s and 1930s. The sheer scale and variety of O'Neill's materials demanded new theatre and in turn made exciting, ambitious demands on actors, designers, directors and audiences. But he remained a *popular* dramatist, such were the excellent conditions of American theatre before the Second World War. Indeed O'Neill's 1920s plays – *The Emperor Jones* and *The Hairy Ape*, for example, would not be unfamiliar in their expressionist techniques: use of different stage levels and the auditorium itself, of dance, masks and music – especially popular forms of what was broadly called jazz – and a variety of verbal forms.

The one-act play *Hughie*, 1940, exemplifies O'Neill's skills. It is virtually a monologue which reveals the life of the speaker, Erie Smith, a gambler, and of the man about whom he tells his stories, the dead Hughie. But the action also presents Smith's sole auditor – apart from the theatre audience – Charlie, the night clerk of the small New York hotel, the play's location – 'between 3 and 4 a.m. of a day in the summer of 1928'. Charlie is largely built in O'Neill's stage-directions: extensive, detailed instructions for an actor, and for a reader. Off-stage sounds project part of the cold-lonely boredom of city existence, from which Erie, given as 'a teller of tales', is an obsessed and obsessive relief. For 45 minutes, O'Neill organises his gift for language – Erie's is American authentic speech, localised and dated. But the stage directions indicate O'Neill's primary desire for theatre: to play into it the third-person narrative complexity of the novel; to enrich drama by liberating it from traditions of over-simplicity and worn-out theatre conventions. He produces a text with a complexity of materials and reference on which director and actor have to work with their skill, and work hard. The text needs a soundtrack to present Charlie's thoughts and responses and film to project the city location – what was later to be called a mixed-media production. *Hughie* draws on O'Neill's downtown New York experiences of 1915 – in fact, some of the language has been identified as 1915 rather than 1928, and a decrepit Greenwich Village saloon-hotel called the Golden Swan, known by its clientele as the Hell Hole – famous enough to be painted by John Sloan and Charles Demuth. O'Neill used it for one of his finest plays, *The Iceman Cometh*, in 1946.[16]

In these plays, as with another late masterpiece, *Long Day's Journey into Night* (1941), the language techniques are existential – that is, the characters talk for dear life – survival talk, especially monologue for compulsive revelation. One of the theatre sources is Maxim Gorky's *Lower Depths* (1902) – the Russian playwright whom Mark Twain was delegated to welcome to America. Another source is long confessional speech in Strindberg. Language takes on an almost physical compulsion, a human device for differentiation and assertion which is itself deeply dramatic and penetrative.

O'Neill was well aware of the difficulties of transferring American speech to the rhetorical levels demanded by an action such as, for example, *Mourning Becomes Electra*, his trilogy of 1929 to 1931, with its triple intensity drawn from Greek tragedy, American history and Freudian psychoanalysis. He needed, he once said, 'great language to lift it beyond itself. I haven't got that.' O'Neill's plays, as a whole, use a strong variety of American language. There *are* pages where the *writing* appears to be awkward, especially where he needs direct philosophical and psychological ideas. But in general practice, with attention by actors and direction, his language works as *theatre* action. The distinguished theatre director and critic Harold Clurman repeatedly claimed this to be the case, and we have many experiences of it in recent productions. One of the finest O'neill actors, Jason Robards, says that O'Neill wrote plays 'to be performed. He didn't write literature.' Actors in fact do not speak of O'Neill's deficiencies, but say how the language is a flexible and highly usable vehicle in his best plays.

He knew that his continuous problem was to find forms for the complexity of his vision, that he had to invent and experiment continually with producing a performance text, a theatre text, and a text which extended the boundaries of theatre transactions between performers and audience. His American expressionism combines visual and plastic arts, sound and music, language and fiction, and controlled movement into his own forms. His stage directions early in his career became a set of controls towards total ends – to control theatre in his own creativity, prior to performance; to control the signs and the signified into a performance text. But it is the stage performance that is the complex order of sign controls: there are no accidents. As the Austrian playwright Peter Handke says, 'there is a theatrical reality going on at each moment. A chair on the stage is a theatre chair.'[17]

O'Neill mastered such transformations and transactions – the theatre codes, the languages of theatre components. But his works are also a series of interventions into American society. They are 'an art of explanation' as well as 'an art of expression', in which 'the techniques of the stage are themselves "committed" '. He emphasised emotive factors, but in practice he understood 'that the theatrical phenomenon might be treated in cognitive and not purely emotive terms; he was able to conceive the theatre intellectually, abolishing the (stale but tenacious) mythic distinction between . . . the "heart" and the "head"; his theatre is neither pathetic nor cerebral: it is *justified* theatre'.[18] Those terms are Roland Barthes's for Brecht, but they suit O'Neill remarkably, and in the 1930s and 1940s. Barthes also speaks to another set of techniques that O'Neill tackled: to produce '*consciousness of unconsciousness*, consciousness the audience must have of the unconsciousness prevailing on the stage . . . to show that the world is an object to be deciphered . . . a theatre of the signifier'.[19]

The power of *Long Day's Journey* lies with that sense of consciousness and unconsciousness before a contemplative and therefore active audience, whose witnessing silence is itself an embodiment of consciousness–unconsciousness transactions. In addition, James Tyrone, in this play, is an actor being acted – the *Hamlet* materials are fully present. O'Neill's stage directions say: 'the actor shows in all his unconscious habits of speech, movement and gesture'. But all four members of the Tyrone family enact in this interface, and within a soundtrack of fog-horns – sounds for concealment and danger – within a musical repetition of phrase and memories, within an enclosed, theatrical confrontation of familiar signs, rhythmic patterns of blame, recognition and attempts at love. The presence of the great actor, Edwin Booth, in James Tyrone's memory, is itself part of a reliance on performance tradition – a security of theatre, the use of mask and persona to live.

Many years earlier, in 1916, the seamen's quarters in *Bound East for Cardiff* presented enclosure within voyage, language within claustrophobia, the sea enclosure on the move – with the dream of a farm as remote stabiliser. In *The Long Voyage Home* (1916–17), a seaman's desire is revealed in the dream of a Swedish farm; and often revealed under drunkenness, when masks fall and systems of protection dissolve, and the audience become voyeurs of the private, O'Neill's people struggle to become sufficiently conscious. In *Desire Under the Elms* (1924), he removes the walls of the three rooms of a farmhouse to reveal a place of concealed desire. O'Neill's father, himself an actor, said after a performance of *Beyond the Horizon* in 1920: 'What are you trying to do – send them home to commit suicide?'

The drum soundtrack that encloses the black Brutus Jones in *The Emperor Jones* of 1920, the forest as the enclosure of his 'Little Formless Fears', the presence of a slave ship, the sound of the wind, the

Witch Doctor's sounds, the revolver shots – this is O'Neill's programme of tension to dramatise the nightmares of guilt in his main
figure. Beneath the mask of his 'robes and furred gowns', beneath
'the surface of the river ... unruffled in the moonlight', inside the
jungle – lies the 'behind life', edging, as usual in O'Neill, into the
primal space of human beings. He may have written the first significant part for a black actor, but beyond 'black' lies the human,
the existential, the private, the primal, as it does in Conrad's African Congo centre.

Yank Smith, in *The Hairy Ape* (1921), is first enclosed in a ship's
stokehold, expressionistically presented to the audience, and at last
enclosed in the cage of an ape. Both Jones and Smith in the commonplace of the names enact what O'Neill takes to be – are *popularly*
taken to be – commonplaces of the bases of action; and again in
1925 with Brown in *The Great God Brown*. These men desire to be
something beyond their enclosure, but are shown returning to a
primal level which is death to the human. Yank's stokehold, seamen's
quarters, prison and cage become scenes of awareness, loneliness
and quest. But the enclosure of class, labour and race are not tran-
scended. These are not social protest plays to lead to social change.
O'Neill wrote to Kenneth Macgowan that his theatre techniques
'run the whole gamut from extreme naturalism to extreme expressionism – with more of the latter than the former'.[20] But those methods are designed to produce anxieties of limitation in an audience.
He is a popular middle-class playwright. In *All God's Chillun Got
Wings* (1923), the white Ella Downey plunges her knife into a Congo
mask – but the play shows the limitation of her black husband
through race prejudice:

Nigger Jim Harris – become a full-fledged Member of the Bar?
... It'd be against all natural laws, all human rights and justice.

In Act I, scene iv, Jim and Ella have to pass 'two racial lines ... rigid
and unyielding, staring across at each other with bitter hostile eyes'.
In Act II, scene ii, another enclosure: their rooms walls 'appear
shrunken in, the ceiling lowered, so that the furniture, the portrait,
the mask look unnaturally large and domineering'. The elemental
enclosure for *Desire under the Elms* – and O'Neill had been consider-
ing Euripides' *Hippolytus* and *Medea* – is a sign of bases in fate and
determinism:

Two enormous elms are on each side of the house . . . They appear to protect and at the same time subdue. There is a sinister maternity in their aspect, a crushing, jealous absorption.

Desire acts under oppression in the primal mode – the Californian Gold Rush, the Father worshipping a stony God the Father, the dead mother, the farm's rooms to be possessed and owned: these boundaries are broken by sexual union outside law and society. The elms and the land are visibly present against a farmhouse seen as home *under law*. O'Neill's imitation of rural speech is itself a dialect of enclosure, of limitation – emotional, repetitive, developed by non-verbal gestures more powerful than ideas. Emotion *exceeds* language, and breaks the closure – just as Yank's speech breaks his sense of deprivation.

In *The Great God Brown*, gaps in behaviour and consciousness lie under actual masks – signs of division between desires, in the social, between private and social, what is controlled and what resists control, what is law and what is illegal, but necessary under desire. Dion Anthony's name includes Dionysian or Nietzschean emotional releases and the Christian myth of erotic temptation. His mask shows a public behaviour – cynical and mocking. His 'behind life' is his face – 'spiritual' and almost childlike. The public surface is security against family, society, the daily survival struggle – a protective enclosure against enclosure, a schizophrenic security against the assumed weakness of friendship with William Brown, the American businessman, and his love for Margaret. Margaret is herself masked as a socially required female image, she presents both security and vulnerability. It is while wearing Dion's mask that Brown is killed at the end of the play. Social necessities demand masks; the self is caged. O'Neill's assumption is that there is a primal self. At on point he directs that Dion 'clasps on his mask in a terrible effort of will', in panic; and then he is torn in agony as he wears it. His face becomes 'furrowed with pain and torture'. Margaret refuses to recognise him without his social-success mask. The patterns of alienation are given through expressionist device. Dion masks his need for God and for his art: 'Why was I born without a skin, O God, that I must wear armour in order to touch and be touched?' William Brown's business success masks failure in emotion. The structure of controlling class is deconstructed as personal limitation *within* the system's necessities. It is a 1920s action of frustration, contemporary with the fictions of Sinclair Lewis and Theodore

Dreiser – the plot of the sensitive American against business materialism, rebel against reformer and Fitzgerald's concerns with the failure of nourishment. The outcome is sacrificial. In *Days Without End*, completed in 1933 in the middle of the Depression, John Loving is divided into two figures played by two actors: John and Loving. Loving has the same age, height, hair and dress. O'Neill's directions require that:

> [his] face is a mask whose features reproduce exactly the features of John's face – the death mask of a John who has died with a sneer of scornful mockery on his lips. And this mocking scorn is repeated in the expression of the eyes which stare bleakly from behind the mask.

That mask is also described as 'Mephistophelian' – the satanic mocker of tradition. When John is writing, 'his features automatically assume the meaningless affable expression which is the American business man's welcoming poker face'. He calls his public self 'a malignant spirit hiding behind life' in order to catch people 'in their hour of happiness'. But beyond his awareness, writes O'Neill, he is 'trapped like an animal in a cage'.

Then O'Neill goes a stage further. The figure of religious faith, as an alternative to defeat, Father Matthew Baird, resembles John and Loving externally, but 'his appearance and personality radiate health and observant kindness – also the confident authority of one who is accustomed to obedience and deference . . . an unshakeable calm and certainty, the peace of one whose goal in life is fixed by an end beyond life'. A figure, then, to challenge lack of confidence and meaning, major themes of 1930s' American writing. Authority had been exposed as a force for the collapse of America's capitalist confidence, eroded into depair and the deaths of thousands by starvation and suicide. Where the Left attempted to convince Americans of an alternative society, O'Neill's atavism moved back – as T. S. Eliot's hunt for an available past moved back to a vision of Christendom. The saloon derelicts of Harry's place in *The Iceman Cometh*, six years later in 1939, are not even offered these prescriptions. They are compelled to retain their masks, their pipedream illusions, as O'Neill dubs them, their dreams of a possible life, the haunted sense of an opportunity untaken.

Back in 1926 O'Neill had composed *Lazarus Laughed*, his most extended vision of a performance text, a large-scale complex of choreographic controls, musical environment, hundreds of actors in 400 costumes and 300 masks representing the seven ages of man, seven types of character and three races. The materials are the possibility of rebirth or rejuvenation – a characteristically American region of desire. The form is a huge revivalist communalism – a highly American occasion – in multi-media. O'Neill called it 'A Play for the Imaginative Theatre': an advance which he believed was a return 'to the one true theatre'. Once again, the Dionysian origins of theatre concern him – its function

> as a Temple where the religion of a poetical interpretation and symbolical celebration of life is communicated to human beings starved in spirit by their soul-stifling daily struggle to exist as masks among the masks of living.

The huge cast is masked – except Lazarus. O'Neill's explicitness is deeply related to the increased twentieth-century apprehension of the masses, moving towards the totalitarian, between the two world wars:

> In masking the crowds . . . I was visualizing an effect that, intensified by dramatic lighting, would give an audience visually the sense of the Crowd, not as a random collection of individuals, but as a collective whole, an entity. When the Crowd speaks, I wanted an audience to hear the voice of the Crowd mind, Crowd emotion, as one voice of a body composed of, but quite distinct from, its parts.[21]

The Crowd, the masses, the mob, the collective – this had already become a powerful force by 1926, a severe manifestation of the People, and a peculiarly American version of this ambiguous term, especially within a highly ambivalent capitalist democracy. Once again, O'Neill's theatre technique transacts a social idea. The one individual is a man who has penetrated death and returned, but can communicate this unique experience only by joyful, freed laughter: ecstatic confidence as against hopeless fear of life through fearing death and the forces of repression, the affirmative 'yes' but only in speechless laughter.

The Nietzschean–Dionysian impulse is again present, in O'Neill's sense of a fertilizing energy, that life-force which haunted Henri Bergson, Bernard Shaw, D. H. Lawrence and other writers, through

to Norman Mailer's essay 'The White Negro' in 1957. O'Neill tackled the myth of it in *The Fountain* in 1921 – the fifteenth-century
search for the fountain of youth in Florida by one Juan Ponce de
Leon, who is led to it by an Indian (the primal) and is ambushed,
and mortally wounded. In his delirium he sees his beloved Beatriz,
hears the song of the fountain and accepts its message – the 'eternal
becoming' in the life-force of which he is already a part. His dying
words are: 'O Fountain of Eternity, take back this drop, my soul!'
Five years later, Lazarus, out of Christian myth, works with what
O'Neill called 'the first theatre that sprang, by virtue of man's
imaginative interpretation of life, out of his worship of Dionysus'.

The aphoristic, exclamatory, prophesying language is in part
drawn from Nietzsche's *Thus Spake Zarathustra*, which O'Neill kept
beside his bed to read. But the centre is a laugh – a peculiarly
human sound, and non-verbal as well as non-animal, that has to be
interpreted. What *has* Lazarus discovered? It is in his laugh. Again,
O'Neill was aware of his problem in theatre, writing to Kenneth
MacGowan:

> Who can we get to laugh as one would laugh who had com-
> pletely lost, even from the depths of the unconscious, all traces of
> the Fear of Death? . . . In short, *Lazarus* is damned far from any
> category. It has no plot of any sort as one knows plot . . . I had
> better stop getting more involved in explaining what I can't, for
> the present, explain to myself.[22]

There speaks the creative artist in the precise mode of risking ar-
ticulation, the playwright of 'a theatre of the imagination unbound
and one in which the audience especially might participate more
vitally and fully'.[23] He spoke to Paul Green, an American playwright
especially concerned with collective, epic theatre, about his idea of
a *Lazarus* production in which – and it reminds us directly of the
productions of the Living Theatre in the 1960s – 'the audience [would
be] caught up enough to join in the responses – the laughter and
chorus statements even – much as Negroes do in one of their revival
meetings'.[24] The work was in fact produced in 1927 in California –
O'Neill thought 'successfully and imaginatively' – and later at
Fordham University in New York, but never on Broadway; and
there is no film record of these performances.

By 1929 O'Neill's dream of a theatre of origins had become a
version of dammed up life, repetition, of eternal inheritance of

determinism, rather than an eternal opportunity for life in the new.
In the working notes for *Mourning Becomes Electra*, O'Neill writes,
in April 1929, that he chose to substitute for Aeschylus' Trojan War
location a war nearer to Americans but not as near as the First
World War – the Civil War of 1860–5: an event known, distant and
historically present; and in theatre terms

> possessing costume . . . possessing sufficient mask of time and
> space, so that audiences will unconsciously grasp at once, it is
> primarily drama of hidden life forces – fate – behind lives of
> characters . . . Civil War as a background for drama of murder-
> ous family love and hate –

So *Mourning Becomes Electra* brings together O'Neill's major components, a masking revelatory tragedy, placing America in the
European tradition and legitimation. The dynastic destiny design
enters the New World, and the immediate structures are conse-
quently controlled, as they are in William Faulkner's *Absalom,
Absalom!* and T. S. Eliot's *The Family Reunion* – the Oedipal family
drama focused through history and religion. In O'Neill's play,
American Greek-style architecture would enable the Mannon house
to be a 'New England House of Atreus', wrote O'Neill, and within
it the 'Greek plot of crime and retribution, chain of fate' would be
the 'Puritan conviction of man born to sin and punishment'. Inside
the plot and architecture mask, family resemblances would be visually held by *facial* similarity – O'Neill initially contemplated the use
of masks, then half masks, and finally make-up as mask: 'the death-
mask-like expression of characters' faces in repose being suddenly
torn open by panic'. O'Neill is still working the theatre of *The Great
God Brown* and *Days Without End*. But the Strindbergian sense of
'behind-life' is to be given in a more extensive way: 'the unreal
behind what we call reality which is the real reality! – the unrealistic
truth wearing the mask of lying reality'. But there is to be no masking
through imitation of past speech forms – 'Stick to modern temper
of dialogue without pretence of Civil War lingo', he notes.

These 'Working Notes' show O'Neill deep into possible uses of
mask, soliloquy, asides, formal and commonplace speech, and other
theatre techniques, with a degree of consciousness emerging from
long experience of practical theatre – sound and visual presentation for a public occasion, a multiple action, and a multiple that
expressionist theatre had offered: 'the stage' as *all* sight and sound

resources, the non-verbal and verbal interfused, towards a range of social and psychological revelations. His experience *in the theatre* of Yeats and Synge by the Abbey Theatre, performances of Ibsen, and other occasions, were incorporated into his own inventions and experimentations far beyond current commercial American theatre practice. Between 1914 and 1943, he created a body of theatre performance texts whose formal inventiveness is unrivalled, and yet he believed that he worked in a failed society and that his work exemplified it. In 1946, during an interview at the Theatre Guild, O'Neill said,

> The United States, instead of being the most successful country in the world is the greatest failure . . . because it was given everything more than any other country . . . Its main idea is that everlasting game of trying to possess your own soul by the possession of something outside it too.[25]

In a letter, he saw his function clearly, and it is characteristic in his generation of American writers:

> to see the transfiguring nobility of tragedy, in as near the Greek sense as one can grasp it . . . I am always conscious of the Force behind – Fate, God, our biological past creating our present, whatever one calls it – Mystery certainly.[26]

He had the ability to create examples for that transfiguration. Mary McCarthy put it well in 1946, after experiencing *The Iceman Cometh*: 'made of ice and fire; it is full of will and fanatical determination; it appears to have hardened at some extreme temperature of mind'.[27]

In *More Stately Homes*, O'Neill for one last time penetrates the schizophrenia of the cultural failure he sensed. In the early nineteenth-century American of President Jackson, Deborah Harford drives her son to burn his Utopian writings and plunge into *laissez-faire* monopolies and the slave trade. But then Simon's rebellion begins to move:

> It's as if I no longer had the strength to hold myself together. Another 'me' is in revolt – is freeing itself – as if from this moment on I had to be two 'me's' – a state of war.

It is that issue of freedom that the Hungarian politician, philoso-
pher and student of literature, Georg Lukács, reached mostly finely,
into the energy centre of O'Neill's large life work, when he wrote
in 1957 of his contemporaneity – and it can lead us towards an
understanding of the reasons why his plays are still steadily produced today. Lukács at this point has been placing Ibsen in European moral drama:

> The ethical-dramatic dialectic is no longer that between absolute
> imperatives and the impossibility of their realization. We are now
> concerned with the scope and possibilities of human action as
> such; O'Neill's subject is man himself, his subjectively tragic and
> yet objectively comic situation . . . The America he portrays is,
> sociologically, that described by his contemporaries – though often,
> to win dramatic distance, he sets the scene in the America of the
> past. But he is interested not so much in the way human beings
> can be manipulated in the name of 'Freedom', as in whether, and
> how, the human substance can survive such a process. O'Neill
> wishes to know whether a man is in the last analysis respons-
> ible for his own actions or is the plaything of psychological and
> social forces over which he has no control . . . O'Neill's originality
> [is that] seeing the situation as he does, he is yet able to affirm,
> with his own brand of tragicomic defiance, a basic integrity in
> human personality . . . at the same time a protest against the domi-
> nance of modernism and a confession of faith in the future of
> humanity.[28]

NOTES

1. All quotes are taken from Eugene O'Neill, *The Plays of Eugene O'Neill* (New York: Random House, 1954).
2. Arthur and Barbara Gelb, *O'Neill* (London: Jonathan Cape, 1962) p. 537.
3. Ibid.
4. Eugene O'Neill, 'Strindberg and Our Theatre', in Horst Frenz (ed.), *American Playwrights on Drama* (New York: Hill & Wang, 1965).
5. Ibid.
6. Roland Barthes, *Critical Essays* (Evanston, Ill.: Northwestern University Press, 1972) p. 66.
7. W. B. Yeats, 'From "Oedipus at Colonnus" ', in *Collected Poems* (London: Macmillan, 1930) p. 255.

8. Jack London, in Willard Thorpe, *American Writing in the Twentieth Century* (Cambridge, Mass.: Harvard University Press, 1960) p. 162.
9. Louis Sheaffer, *O'Neill: Son and Artist* (Boston, Mass.: Little, Brown, 1973) p. 306.
10. Gelb, *O'Neill*, p. 871.
11. John Henry Raleigh (ed.), *The Iceman Cometh: A Collection of Critical Essays* (Englewood Cliffs, N.J.: Prentice-Hall, 1968) p. 20.
12. Eugene O'Neill, correspondence.
13. Mary Heaton Vorse, *Time and a Town: A Provincetown Chronicle* (New York: Dial Press, 1942) p. 142.
14. Willard Thorpe, *American Writing in the Twentieth Century* (Cambridge, Mass.: Harvard University Press, 1960) pp. 69, 73ff.
15. Ibid., p. 79.
16. Gelb, *O'Neill*, pp. 87–90, 284–5.
17. Peter Handke, 'Nauseated by Language' (an interview), *Drama Review*, no. 15 (1970).
18. Barthes, *Critical Essays*, pp. 38, 262.
19. Ibid., p. 263.
20. Sheaffer, *O'Neill*, p. 172.
21. Gelb, *O'Neill*, p. 601.
22. Ibid.
23. Ibid., p. 602.
24. Ibid.
25. Ibid., p. 870.
26. Eric Bentley, 'Trying to Like O'Neill', in *In Search of Theatre* (New York: Vintage Books, 1954).
27. Mary McCarthy, 'Eugene O'Neill – Dry Ice', in *Sights and Spectacles, 1937–58* (London: Heinemann, 1959).
28. Georg Lukács, *The Meaning of Contemporary Realism* (London: Merlin Press, 1962) pp. 83–4.

3
Clifford Odets
MICHAEL WOOLF

One day Cheryl Crawford, one of the Group's directors, asked me to read half a dozen scripts which were being considered for production. I went through them with little interest, until I came to the last, whose vivid characterization, pungent dialogue and effective dramaturgy revealed a brilliant new talent . . . The play was *Awake and Sing!*, by Clifford Odets.[1]

Elmer Rice's judgement was fairly representative in the mid 1930s. In contrast, Margaret Gibson recorded the tone of the obituaries that followed Odets's death in 1963:

The newspapers and magazines with few exceptions printed obituaries which were strangely personal, some faintly accusatory, others supercilious; almost all were offhand.[2]

By the 1960s Odets's writing had been largely forgotten and his intellectual and liberal reputation had been bruised by his willingness to testify to the House Committee on Un-American Activities in 1952. For a few years in the 1930s Clifford Odets had enjoyed popular and critical success. In one year, 1935, in a surge of creative energy, Odets completed four plays that were produced by the Group theatre company. The plays were *Waiting for Lefty*, *Awake and Sing!*, *Paradise Lost*, *Till the Day I Die*.[3] Much of his critical reputation came out of those plays and depends to a degree on the perceived value of that year's work. Such a view is a distortion and simplification of what is, in reality, a complex career.

Odets's career has been made murky by a number of myths through which he has tended to be seen. In the first of these, he is placed firmly in the context of the proletarian literature movement of the 1930s. In fact, only a one-act play, *Waiting for Lefty*, can be wholly placed in the context of agit-prop theatre. Indeed, few of Odets's characters are of a strictly proletarian background. More commonly they are drawn from the lower-middle and middle classes. Odets never had a coherent ideological basis in his plays beyond a generalised concern for the impoverished, what Leslie Fiedler calls 'sentimental radicalism', and a desire to represent 'ordinary' people in a serious manner.[4] Harold Clurman knew Odets's work as a director and as a founder of the Group theatre:

> There was in it a fervour that derived from the hope and expectation of change and the desire for it. But there was rarely any expression of political consciousness in it, no deep commitment to a coherent philosophy of life, no pleading for a panacea. 'A tendril of revolt' runs through all of Odets' work, but that is not the same thing as a consistent revolutionary conviction.[5]

In part, the reading of Odets as a kind of ideologue of the 1930s Left is, as Arthur Miller indicates, a symptom of the radical imperatives of the times,

> As always, we were trapped into estimating writers by what they apparently stood for rather than by what they were actually doing, by the critical propaganda surrounding them rather than by their literary deeds.[6]

From a current perspective, Odets's political radicalism appears to be rhetorical addition to the plays, a flourish that often has little or no organic place in the dramatic developments portrayed on the stage. More often than not they arise in moments of forced epiphany. The meanings of the work appear beyond and beneath the virtually obligatory rhetoric of the 1930s Left.

The other myth that serves to distort his significance is that of Hollywood. The notion that Hollywood is destructive of the creative writer and that Odets is (another) victim of that process is used to explain what is perceived as creative failure post-1940. There is a common association often made between Hollywood and wealth and the death of creativity that is used, by Arthur Miller for example, as a means of neatly categorising Odets's experience. 'What had he been doing in Hollywood but wasting his talent making money?'[7] This view contains two potential distortions. The first is that Odets's creativity dried up after 1940. While Odets certainly produced less for the theatre, he wrote extensively for the cinema and, in 1948, produced *The Big Knife* which, in Edward Murray's view, is one of

Odets's most important works: '*The Big Knife* is a powerful drama
– disturbing, wild and unforgettable – something which comes when
an artist has driven his vision to an extreme.'[8]

The other notion that Hollywood somehow weakened Odets's
creative power ignores the fact that, ostensibly at least, Odets
was enthusiastic about the positive impact of working in the film
industry. 'What the critics don't realize is that I picked up half
my techniques here ... The movies are a brilliant training school
for a dramatic writer.'[9]

There may also be some tendency to see *The Big Knife* as autobiographical in some sense or other. Whatever the source, a common view is that Hollywood had, in combination with other factors,
somehow sapped his energies as an author. Joseph Wood Krutch's
view is representative of a number of similar perspectives:

> Odets's *The Big Knife* and *The Country Girl*[10] reflected the author's
> new life as a Hollywood scenarist and though they attracted
> renewed attention to a writer with great theatrical talent neither
> had the strong individuality which first distinguished him.[11]

However, a number of other factors combined at the end of the
1930s to undermine those conditions that had encouraged Odets's
creativity. On a personal level, a failed marriage enforced a thread
of bitterness which became manifest in *Clash by Night* (1941). On a
more political level, the outbreak of war signalled the failure of
1930s radicalism to alter the world in ways imagined in the rhetoric
of the times. Above all, perhaps, the Group theatre disbanded.

Odets's early career was shaped by the Group theatre and the
years of its existence, from 1930 to 1940, coincided with the years
of his greatest productivity:

> To some degree ... the fate of the company and of this writer
> were entwined. It was the success of his plays in 1935 which
> cemented the success of the company and it was the gradual
> disengagement of the company from his 1941 play, *Clash by Night*,
> which marked its dissolution.[12]

Odets's talent was nurtured and nourished by the Group and his
plays were profoundly influenced by his experiences there. He
recognised this fact in an interview in 1961: 'Without the Group
Theatre I doubt that I would have become a playwright.'[13]

The founders, Lee Strasberg, Harold Clurman and Cheryl Craw-ford, together created what was close to a commune or commun-ity of actors and writers:

> Their primary aims were to establish new and more vital rela-tions between actor and author, between actor and actor, and above all, between the authors and the society in which they lived. They were not committed to social and political radicalism, especially at the start, but were in search of serious, non escap-ist scripts, preferably with social implications. Only by living, rehearsing, discussing, working and thinking together – they felt – could they realize the full possibilities of a permanent acting company and as a result achieve in their productions greater unity and more significant social connotations.[14]

The formal objectives of the group coincided with Odets's view of what constituted the purpose and meaning of theatre while the community gave him personal support and affirmation in contrast to what had been an unhappy, even suicidal, childhood and youth. He has been described as 'happier and more secure in the collective life of the Group than he had ever been in the booming twenties'.[15] Harold Clurman gives some indication of the life-style of the Group theatre:

> We were all living in remarkable fashion. At least half the Group had moved into a ten-room flat on West Fifty-Seventh Street near the railroad tracks. The rent was fifty dollars a month, for besides its unfavourable location, the house was a neglected old brown-stone with insufficient heat and a generally damp atmosphere.
> Meals were provided for through a common fund, marketing was done by the two girls, and the cooking was attended to in turn by four or five of the men who had a knack for it. Clifford Odets's virtuosity in this field was confined to potato pancakes and hot chocolate . . .[16]

The collapse of the Group in 1940 can, with the other political and personal matters, offer a coherent explanation for the relative decline in Odets's productivity that is at least as convincing as the Hollywood myth.

In any case, it is clear that there are alternative contexts through which his writing can be viewed. In this chapter, a number of perspectives will be offered on the significance and meanings of Odets's work which will balance both the excessive critical enthusiasm of the 1930s and the subsequent neglect from the 1950s onwards. The discussions will indicate how, in one view, Odets can be read within the context of Jewish-American literature of the period. *Awake and Sing!*, for example, represents a recurrent theme in Jewish-American writing of the transformed family structure. The secularisation of family life leads inexorably to the diminution of patriarchal authority, traditionally associated with the function of a religious head of the family. One impact of this process of transformation is to create an emergent mother, a Bessie Berger figure, as the central force of the family. In other ways, Odets reflects Jewish-American experience: in the use of Yiddish-English as a dramatic language; in the emphasis on father–son relationships and the conflict between generations; in the expression of a secularised version of a Messianic myth as a form of socialist Utopianism.

Odets can also be read in the context of Romantic literature in so far as he creates a sequence of characters longing for some idealised version of experience. That these idealised images are frequently distorted into crassly commercial shapes reveal Odets as a social critic of a commercialised, acquisitive, consumer society. He was not, however, a simple realist. Many of the plays work through contrasting metaphorical structures, use epiphany as a catalyst, and they construct sequences of action followed by consequences that bring the whole closer to didactic fabulation than realism. The symbolic conflict between the violin and boxing in *Golden Boy* and Joe's death belong more to moral fable than the randomness of reality. The conflicting models of suicide and birth, employed and reemployed in many of the plays, is similarly a structure owing much to fable.

The Depression is the filter through which much experience is recorded. Fears and insecurities bred in the 1930s persist throughout Odets's plays and become a part of his perception of human experience: a permanent state of unease. In another respect, Odets reflects the legacy of the 1930s in, for example, *The Big Knife*, where Hollywood success is seen as a kind of double betrayal of both the values of the theatre and an earlier radicalism. In another sense, *Golden Boy* draws upon boxing in two respects: as a popular theme in the movies of the time and as a pathway to self-improvement for young men in immigrant communities with little access to the more conventional channels of advancement.

Odets needs to be seen, as the following discussion of the plays themselves indicates, both as a representational figure whose concerns and methods of expression are symptomatic of the times and as a playwright whose work sought to address broad issues of human behaviour, passion and aspiration. This chapter considers Odets within the context of Jewish-American writing, with regard to his treatment of love and aspiration, as a form of American Romantic, and in relation to the economic, cultural and political experiences of the 1930s.

The tendency to categorise Odets as a writer contained and bounded by the 1930s distorts the real value of the work which encompasses the emotional signs of those nightmarish times but goes beyond them. The significance of this work is, primarily, in the combination of a quasi-Romantic perception with a social concern for immigrant experience perceived through a Jewish-American consciousness formed in a time of turmoil.

Waiting for Lefty (first produced 1935) was unashamedly an agit-prop production. It is also the only play by Odets that is unarguably a political drama with a clear radical intention. Interest in it now is primarily historical. It was presented in a double bill with *Till the Day I Die*, which similarly has historical rather than dramatic interest. It is an early example of anti-Nazi theatre. Together, these two plays offer an insight into the domestic and international preoccupations of American radicals in the mid-1930s and contain a few signals of the issues and techniques that Odets was to develop in further plays. The use of contrasting motifs of suicide and birth as dichotomies reflecting despair and hope is characteristic of Odets's dramatic strategy and is first expressed in *Till the Day I Die*. Scene iv concludes with the Major's suicide while scene v opens with the announcement by the young woman, Tilly, of her pregnancy. It is presented explicitly as a sign of optimism and hope in the future:

> TILLY: Till the day we die there is steady work to do. Let us hope we will both live to see strange and wonderful things. Perhaps we will die before then. Our children will see it then. Ours!
> ERNST (*bitterly*):   Our children!
> TILLY: I'm going to have a baby, Ernst . . .[17]

Waiting for Lefty demonstrates the talent Odets was to refine later with regard to the use of shifting registers. An easy transition from everyday speech to a rhetoric that builds on everyday speech patterns but elevates them towards a language of poetry signals Odets's political objectives: to elevate the language of the poor and, thereby, to suggest the potential for nobility in the dispossessed. Odets's dramatic language affirms the importance of the experiences of the poor and the exploited. Art is made out of everyday experience and this also, clearly, relates to Odets's general political sympathies. The play was also interesting in that it was constructed precisely to be presented in any hall. It required no scenery or special theatrical device. In short, it was an attempt at a play about, for and by an economic and social group rarely served by the theatre of the times.

Far more interesting than these two plays, however, was *Awake and Sing!* (1935). It was, in fact, the first play written by Odets though it was produced later in the year. It was a skilful play that raised issues of greater complexity and interest than those presented in the politically driven plays *Waiting for Lefty* and *Till the Day I Die*.

Awake and Sing! is Odets's first exploration of tension and disintegration within the family. The Berger family is dominated by the mother, Bessie, who prefigures the satirical monster-mothers of the 1960s who found vivid expression in comic form, particularly in novels such as Philip Roth's *Portnoy's Complaint*, Wallace Markfield's *Teitelbaum's Window*, Bruce Jay Friedman's *A Mother's Kisses* and, in a comic essay, Dan Greenburg's *How to be a Jewish Mother*.

The figure of Bessie reflects the secularisation of Jewish-American family life and a subsequent shift of authority from the father to the mother, the male to the female. Authority traditionally resided in the male because of the father's predominant role as religious head of the household. This invested in the male figure a moral authority and power that shaped roles within the family. The Berger family, like many Jewish-Americans, was secularised and, as a consequence, the patriarchal figures become impotent or comic or defeated. The grandfather Jacob is, as the name signifies, a quasi-patriarchal figure whose power exists only in rhetoric. His rages, remnants of power, are ineffective and treated as inconsequential.

All the fathers in the play are ineffectual figures without clear function. Within the opening seconds Myron, Bessie's husband, is undermined by his daughter:

RALPH: Where's advancement down the place? Work like crazy! Think they see it? You'd drop dead first.

MYRON: Never mind, son, merit never goes unrewarded. Teddy Roosevelt used to say –

HENNIE: It rewarded you – thirty years a haberdashery clerk![18]

The opening exchange reveals both the diminution of the father as a moral authority and the coruscating irony which is typical of the female figures in the Berger family.

Exactly the same inversion of traditional structures is enacted in the relationship between Jacob and Bessie: Jacob is reduced from father to child in a role reversal and distortion that has fatal consequences. This process of family reversal has, certainly, comic potential but it also has, as Odets makes clear, a dimension measured in anguish not only in laughter:

BESSIE: Go in your room, Papa. Every job he ever had he lost because he's got a big mouth. He opens his mouth and the whole Bronx could fall in. Everybody said it –

MYRON: Momma, they'll hear you down the dumbwaiter.

BESSIE: A good barber not to hold a job a week. Maybe you never heard charity starts at home. You never heard it, Pop?

JACOB: All you know, I heard, and more yet. But Ralph you don't make like you. Before you do it, I'll die first. He'll find a girl. He'll go in a fresh world with her. This is a house? Marx said it – abolish such families.

BESSIE: Go in your room, Papa.

JACOB: Ralph you don't make like you!

BESSIE: Go lay in your room with Caruso and the books together.

JACOB: All right!

BESSIE: Go in the room!

JACOB: Some day I'll come out I'll –[19]

Jacob is sent to his room by his daughter, signalling an inversion that is symptomatic of the kinds of pain suffered by the fathers in relation to daughters and wives.

This has, of course, some comic potential and is expressed in the relationship of Hennie with her husband Sam. Sam is a victim of Bessie's plot to make him marry Hennie and accept her child as his own. In the frequent family battles that ensue, Sam, weak, gullible and ineffectual, leaves his home and goes to Bessie's house. Odets puts into Jacob's mouth a commentary on this inversion that is both precise and comic: 'In my day the daughter came home. Now comes the son-in-law.'[20]

Many of the play's themes are reflected in Jacob's exchange with Myron in Act II:

> MYRON: People can't believe in God in Russia. The papers tell the truth, they do.
>
> JACOB: So you believe in God ... you got something for it? You worked for all the capitalists. You harvested the fruits from your labor? You got God! But the past comforts you? The present smiles on you, yes? It promises you the future something? Did you found a piece of earth where you could live like a human being and die with the sun on your face? Tell me, yes, tell me. I would like to know myself. But on these questions, on this theme – the struggle for existence – you can't make an answer. The answer I see in your face ... the answer is your mouth can't talk. In this dark corner you sit and you die. But abolish private property!
>
> BESSIE (*settling the issue*):   Noo, go fight City Hall!
>
> MORTY: He's drunk.[21]

The speech, in the first case, signals the process of secularisation through which the option of God is seen to have become irrelevant and to offer no comfort in the past, present or future. The ironic consequence is to render Jacob powerless except in a rhetorical sense. The absence of God renders the patriarchal voice feeble, without a basis for authority, permitting the dismissive responses of the daughter, Bessie, and the son, Morty.

Furthermore, the speech contains a view of human experience that permeates Odets's work. In short, the Depression is the filter through which Odets perceives human experience throughout most of his writing career. Such a perspective sees existence as a 'struggle' and characterieses life as defined through fear, insecurity, marginality. Characters in *Paradise Lost* (1935), *Golden Boy* (1937), *Rocket to the Moon* (1938) and *Clash by Night* (1941) cling to security at the edge of a precipice and are forced to construct fragile, illusory defences against despair and defeat. The lower-middle-class Bergers or the middle-class Gordons in *Paradise Lost* share a sense that what they have, security and status such as it is, is menaced by forces

outside themselves. Ironically, the stronger characters are the conservative voices like Bessie whose objectives are to maintain what
there is through an essentially stoical rather than activist stance.

Jacob also gives voice to that most American of all dreams for
a 'piece of earth' and a place in the sun. This Edenic vision of a
oneness with nature sits uncomfortably with the actuality of the
experience represented, which is remorselessly urban, where the
only space is upward, on the roof, from where, ultimately, Jacob
jumps to his death. This reveals the extreme fragility of dreams of
alternative experience constructed in the shape of the unattainable.

Throughout Odets's writing characters construct dreams to confront reality. These dreams are in essence of two kinds: they are
either Edenic notions of return to some lost paradise and/or Utopian constructs of some ideal socialist society; or they are 'false
gods', consumer goods and objects into which the characters invest
and accumulate meanings the objects themselves cannot carry.[22]
Within *Awake and Sing!* both kinds of dreams coincide. Sam's wife
Hennie 'looks for a star in the sky' while her brother Ralph gathers
images of what he has been deprived of and invests in them accu-
mulated meanings that reveal the extreme fragility of the dreams.[23]
From a socially critical point of view, they express Odets's implicit
criticism of a society which has translated aspiration into commerce
and possessions. Ralph's discontents are expressed in these forms:
'It's crazy – all my life I want a pair of black and white shoes and
can't get them. It's crazy.'[24] 'I never in my life even had a birthday
party.'[25] 'You never in your life bought me a pair of skates even –
things I died for when I was a kid.'[26]

An exchange between Myron and Bessie precisely captures the
manner in which material objects are elevated into false poetic
alternatives to a harsh actuality. A saxophone and a picture in a
calendar are transformed into magic objects in what is a rare direct
exchange between husband and wife:

MYRON: Yesterday a man wanted to sell me a saxophone with
    pearl buttons. But I –
BESSIE: It's a beautiful picture. In this land, nobody works . . .
    Nobody worries.[27]

It is a moment when the characters come closest to some kind of
nobility, in that real vulnerability is exposed and the humanity
expressed in aspirations that can find neither concrete form nor

complete expression. The visions are impoverished but momentarily achieve the status, poetry and intensity of vision that is, nevertheless, unshared and misplaced. In the construction of such symbols, Odets approaches a Romantic perception of the world.

There are, then, throughout this play, paradises lost and malformed. Bessie destroys Jacob's record of Caruso singing 'O Paradiso'. Moe seeks his paradise with Hennie at the end of the play: 'A certain place where it's moonlight and roses. We'll lay down, count stars.'[28] He offers Hennie (his nickname for her is Paradise) an escape route. The play ends inevitably ambiguously. Hennie seeks this paradise with Moe by abandoning her child. Ralph is symbolically reborn to establish a polarity with Jacob's suicide which re-enacts the dichotomies established in *Till the Day I Die*:

> Did Jake die for us to fight about nickels? No! 'Awake and Sing', he said. Right there he stood and said it. The night he died, I saw he was dead and I was born. I swear to God, I'm one week old![29]

The ambiguities of the play's conclusion contain and modify what might be read as radical optimism. Hennie leaves in pursuit of paradise and Ralph goes nowhere. Images of hope are potential rather than realised and they are formed in shapes that correspond to forms of illusion. It is appropriate that Odets's fourth play of 1935 should have been called *Paradise Lost*.

Paradise Lost, as the preceding discussion suggests, takes many of the themes and issues from *Awake and Sing!* and relocates them in a middle-class context. Fear and insecurity are shown to encompass not just the poorest groups in society. Surprisingly enough, it is Odets's favourite play among those written between 1935 and 1938:

> *Paradise Lost*, poorly received as a practical theatre work, remains my favourite play in this group. While not unmindful of its harsh and ungracious form, I must be permitted to say that our modern audiences, critics included, still must have their plays, like saltwater taffy, cut to fit the mouth. *Paradise Lost* shares with *Rocket to the Moon* a depth of perception, a web of sensory impressions and a level of both personal and social experience not allotted to the other plays here.[30]

This is an odd judgement in that the play thematically adds little to the issues raised in *Awake and Sing!* but is far more impoverished in its language as it loses the verbal energy invested in the speech of the Bergers by the Yiddish-English constructions.

In *Paradise Lost*, 'Odets crams his stage with evidence of collapse and decay'[31] and creates fragile versions of a past seen to contain positive images of promise and hope frustrated in the harsh present. Each of the characters appears to have lost some personal vision of paradise:

> LEO: Clara, my beautiful Clara, what is happening here? Once we were all together and life was good.[32]

For Gus, the paradise was in pre-war America:

> 'I can't explain it to you, Mr. G., how I'm forever hungerin' for the past. It's like a disease in me, eatin' away . . . some nights I have cried myself to sleep . . .'[33]

For all the hopeful rhetoric with which the play concludes, Malcolm Goldstein's summary seems most apt: 'The immigrant's dream of finding an earthly paradise in the new world is seen to have become a nightmare of economic and moral bankruptcy.'[34] In this play, Odets most markedly fails to integrate a political stance with the logic of the play. Leo is bankrupt and without business and home. One of the homeless, Paul, describes Leo's predicament at the conclusion of the play in terms that point to the harshest of realities:

> PAUL: I look at you and see myself seven years back. I been there. This kind of dream paralyzes the will – confuses the mind. Courage goes. Daring goes . . . and in the nights there is sighing. I had my house in the United States. Like you. Did you have a business?
> LEO: Yes.
> PAUL: Like me. you had a sorta little paradise here. Now you lost the paradise. That should teach you something. But no! You ain't awake yet.[35]

Leo's epiphanous vision that 'Heartbreak and terror are not the heritage of mankind!'[36] appears to confirm rather than contradict Paul's assessment. The play does not resolve its contradictions and is, in a sense, redundant in that it replays, in a weaker form, the preoccupations of *Awake and Sing!*

In contrast Odets used new experience for *Golden Boy* (1937). Thematically, the play drew upon the popularity of boxing movies in Hollywood and, indeed, Odets saw the play as something of a money-raiser for the Group. It has much of the structure of a popular fable with the central character choosing between alternatives symbolised as the opposite ends of some kind of spectrum. Joe Bonaparte chooses boxing over the violin and so abandons one set of values, implicitly more cultured and cultivated, for others that are only materialistic. In an increasingly Faustian resonance in Odets's later work, this choice brings him financial reward but also ends in despair, moral defeat and, ultimately, death.

In one sense, the play marked a transition from the earlier to the later plays. The atmosphere of economic unease and material striving is sustained, as are the Romantic projections of a world elsewhere. There is, for example, little or no distinction between Moe's dreamed world at the end of *Awake and Sing!* or Jacob's 'place in the sun' and Lorna's response to Joe's despair in *Golden Boy*:

JOE: But my hands are ruined. I'll never play again! What's left, Lorna? Half a man, useless . . .

LORNA: No, *we're* left! Two together! We have each other! Somewhere there must be happy boys and girls who can teach us the way of life! We'll find some city where poverty's no shame – where music is no crime! – where there's no war in the streets . . .[37]

The characteristics of Odets's later work are also apparent here, particularly in the use of symbol and allegory. For Gabriel Miller, '*Golden Boy* . . . works best as a symbolic play. Odets clearly intended it as an allegory; indeed, he subtitled an earlier draft *An American Allegory*.'[38]

The nature of the allegory is recurrent in the later work. A set of ethics are presented, and figures abandon or betray these in return for financial reward. In *Golden Boy* the ethics betrayed are symbolised in the violin whereas boxing is the symbol for the 'sell-out' to materialism. The contrast is given a more familiar form in *The Big Knife*: theatre versus Hollywood. Harold Cantor summarises this pattern in Odets's work as 'the individual's barter of moral principle for money, power and status'.[39] In these plays, the Faustian element becomes the means through which Odets points the didactic nature of the fable.[40] The protagonists are separated from a version of an elemental self to which, for one reason or another, they are unable to return.

In *Rocket to the Moon* (1938) Odets gave a shape and form to this notion of an elemental self in the figure of Cleo. The influence of Whitman and Emerson has been noted in this aspect of Odets's work and it signals an important shift. The 'salvation' offered in Odets's earliest work was, at least superficially, collective and political from the exhortation to STRIKE at the end of *Waiting for Lefty* to Leo's vision at the end of *Paradise Lost*:

> Everywhere now men are rising from their sleep. Men, men are understanding the bitter black total of their lives. Their whispers are growing to shouts! They become an ocean of understanding! *No man fights alone*.[41]

By *Rocket to the Moon*, the path towards some form of salvation is personal and driven by a notion of discovery of the hidden self that has to be freed. The symbol of singing not only echoes Whitman's, 'I celebrate myself, and sing myself', but is, from *Awake and Sing!* onwards, used to signal this form of personal path towards salvation through perceptions that transcend realities. Escape becomes an act of the imagination as much as physical movement. In the earlier plays the personal co-exists with the political and collective. By *Rocket to the Moon* the individual has become the focus for what is almost a form of transcendental imagination.

In the climax of *Rocket to the Moon*, Cleo is forced to choose between her lovers but the choice she makes is archetypally American and Romantic: for freedom, space, love and the pursuit of joy. All this is symbolised by the idea of singing:

> if there's roads, I'll take them. I'll go up all those roads till I find what I want. I want a love that uses me, that needs me. Don't you think that there's a world of joyful men and women? Must all men live afraid to laugh and sing? Can't we sing at work and love our work? It's getting late to play at life; I want to live it.[42]

In gaining her liberation, she drives Prince and his son-in-law, Stark, to reconciliation and Stark towards a transformed consciousness:

Yes, I, who sat here in this prison-office, closed off from the
world . . . for the first time in years I looked out on the world and
saw things as they really are . . .[43]

For Arthur Miller, *Rocket to the Moon* is Odets's 'one real success
as a writer'.[44] It is apparent that the play looks back towards
Whitman and forwards towards the kinds of transformations that
were to be characteristic of the work of Jack Kerouac, John Clellon
Holmes and the writers who became known a few years later as the
Beats.

In *Night Music: A Comedy in Twelve Scenes* (1940), the two aspects
of Cleo's voice are divided. Rosenberger is 'a partisan of life, liberty
and happiness', the embodiment of an archetypal American view of
the world.[45] Fay Tucker achieves the insight to become another
version of Cleo, a Romantic who articulates the potential to trans-
form and transcend reality: 'Night Music . . . If they can sing, I can
sing. I'm more than them. *We're* more than them. . . . We can sing
through any night.'[46] What is in *Awake and Sing!* a political and
personal response becomes, in this context, an individual vision
of transformation.

In this play Odets also returned to another recurrent theme in
his work. In his introduction to the published edition, Harold
Clurman succinctly summarises Odets's treatment of the theme
of homelessness:

> The play stems from the basic sentiment that people nowadays
> are affected by a sense of insecurity; they are haunted by the fear
> of impermanence in all their relationships; they are fundamentally
> *homeless*, and, whether or not they know it, they are in search of
> a home, of something real, secure, dependable in a slippery,
> shadowy, noisy and nervous world. This search for a home – for
> security of a truly human sort – takes many forms, including the
> comic.[47]

In *Paradise Lost* and *Awake and Sing!*, for example, homelessness was
expressed as a threat in the Depression, where eviction was a real
and present danger. That version exists in *Night Music* but it is more
explicitly broadened into a metaphorical context where what is
missing is both a physical home and a sense of belonging.

Like many of Odets's characters, Steve Takis is from immigrant
stock and this enforces his sense of marginality in relation to

America. The play traces this notion of finding and defining a notion of home and he appeals to the detective Rosenberger to create for him and others like him an America that can offer a sense of location:

> Make this America for me. Make this America for her and her family – they're shivering in their boots. Where is Wilbur Harris? He fell off the freight an' lost a leg. Where's Joe Abrams? Teddy Bannister? In jail. Dan Lowe is pushin' up the daisies – TB. The sweetest little girl on our block – she's peddling it on the streets! An' where are those other pals of my cradle days? Hangin' up by the ears from coast to coast . . . those harmony boys who mighta been! *Make this America for us!*[48]

Rosenberger's role signifies how close Odets gets at time to creating fables. Rosenberger is ostensibly a detective who is about to retire but who is also dying of cancer. In effect, he is a forerunner of J. B. Priestley's inspector in *An Inspector Calls* in that he acts as a *deus ex machina* and as a sage. He protects Steve and Fay, his girlfriend, but guides them towards a version of enlightenment and alternative optimism. Thus he is, even with his Jewish name, a spokesperson for American values as 'a partisan of the pursuit of life, liberty and happiness'. The key significance of Rosenberger is that he embodies a kind of magical synthesis or reconciliation between America and its immigrants. The figure is at once both Jewish moral activist and American sage. He embodies the dual dimensions of Odets's vision in the combination of American vision and Jewish moral consciousness.

At various points, Rosenberger expresses the moral direction of the play and offers commentary on the evolution of events: 'I'll tell you a secret, Miss Tucker. All the dead and living are cheering for you when you are a good person.'[49] In relation to the generational divide treated in the play, he signals a clear commitment to the future and to youth rather than age: 'The function of the parent is to make himself unnecessary. Unfortunately, only animals and birds know it.'[50]

Night Music confronts a number of themes and issues that are recurrent in Odets's work but through a lighter perspective and, at times, in some bizarre contexts; the cause of Steve's problems is the unpredictable behaviour of two performing monkeys he is charged with looking after. This was a departure in tone for Odets and,

certainly, the least realist of all the plays except *The Flowering Peach*
(1954). A reading of that version of the Noah story in conjunction
with *Night Music* focuses attention on the degree to which other,
more ostensibly realist, plays – *Golden Boy* is a clear example – deviate
from realism and move in the direction of fabulation. There is also
in *Night Music* a sustained approach to the issues raised and a
consistency of tone that is not always apparent elsewhere. Harold
Clurman's view is that 'among his longer plays it is the most
integrated in its feeling and the most completely conceived'.[51]

Night Music presents homelessness and isolation in that most
urban, and isolating, of American cities: New York. In this, Winifred
Dusenberry argues that Odets offers a perspective on an archetypal
American condition:

> In one sense Americans are so used to moving that they are never
> homeless and may speak of a casual hotel room as home, but in
> another they are forever homeless, because 'home' is not the place
> where they live, but the place where they lived as a child.[52]

Odets's tone darkened in 1941 in *Clash by Night*, a play clearly
reflecting his matrimonial problems. The play is permeated by discontent. Two couples are contrasted; the married couple, Jerry and
Mae, have a marriage torn by conflict and which ends, finally, in
the murder of Mae's lover.

There are three forms of discontent expressed in the play. In the
first place, the character Peggy expresses a common predicament:
'Great expectations, great disappointments'.[53] Dreams manifestly
exceed the capacity of reality to realise them. Mae's lover Earl exactly
expresses the distance between actuality and aspiration and tells us
that, 'I don't enjoy my life . . . I enjoy only the dream of it.'[54]

Another more concrete discontent derives from the failure of
relationships. Odets's view of married life is almost always marked
by infidelity, tension and emotional isolation. As in *Rocket to the
Moon*, the relationship between husband and wife is desperately
poor but, in this bleak version, no possible reconciliation is pro-
jected. There is a dark vision of isolation in Jerry's view of human
experience:

> You could wake up some day an' find you're an old man with a
> tool kit under your arm an' they don't want you – not even your
> wife. Like my father – my mother didn't speak to him for three
> years before she died.[55]

Mae's view of her marriage enforces the sense of a chasm between aspiration and fulfilment. Her romantic, quasi-heroic dream meets the realities of the human condition:

> I guess I'm a hold-over from another century! Didn't there used to be big, comfortable men? Or was it a dream? Today they're little and nervous, sparrows! But I dream of eagles ... [56]

Mae's comment contains the other form of discontent that runs through the play. In short, to be discontented is seen almost as part of the general human condition, a malaise generated by a form of nostalgia for some version of a mythic, more heroic, past. The play is particularly bleak, and some of Odets's personal unhappiness is manifest in the despair, but *Clash by Night* also endorses Joseph Wood Krutch's assessment:

> No one that I know can more powerfully suggest the essential loneliness of men and women, their inability to explain the varied forms assumed by the symbols of their desire, and the powerlessness of any one of them to help the other. [57]

It was seven years before Odets's work next appeared and, in 1948 and 1950 in *The Big Knife* and *The Country Girl*, he drew upon his own experience in Hollywood and in the theatre for subject matter. [58] *The Big Knife* echoes both *Faust* and *Macbeth* ('Is this a dagger which I see before me?') and revisits many of the concerns previously discussed. It is a moral fable which contains the notion that success betrays past values. To achieve worldly fame and fortune is, in this context, to be damned like Faust and driven, like Macbeth, from one act of betrayal to another:

> Like Macbeth, he is guilty of a series of crimes committed in the pursuit of an ephemeral glory and in defiance of his own higher nature. [59]

The central character is a successful film actor, ironically, in the light of his rootlessness, named Charlie Castle. His wife Marion is the voice of his conscience and the embodiment of the values of the theatre. Exactly like Joe Bonaparte in *Golden Boy*, Charlie is caught between two ends of ethical possibility: theatre versus Hollywood (violin versus boxing). The dichotomy between the two locations is perceived in terms that contrast both ethics and artistic integrity. In that respect, Odets's play belongs within the context of a quasi-genre of anti-Hollywood literature (frequently produced in Hollywood) which includes such disparate works as Nathanael West's novel *The Day of the Locust*, F. Scott Fitzgerald's novel *The Last Tycoon* and includes relatively recent works such as the play *Tales from Hollywood* by Christopher Hampton and the popular musical *City of Angels*.

That aspect of the play is, perhaps, less interesting than the manner in which Odets melds that concern with matters that are expressed elsewhere in his work. The idea of separation from some notion of paradise creates a state of perpetual yearning which approaches Edenic and Zionistic intensity in both Charlie and Marion. Charlie's insight that 'We're homesick all our lives, but adults don't talk about it' signals the kinds of discontent that Odets's characters frequently suffer and that is, as in *Clash by Night*, a symptom of human pain.[60]

The key confrontations in the play are between Charlie and Hank, Marion's lover, who is also, significantly, a writer but who has, in contrast to Charlie, retained his integrity. He is able, therefore, to offer explicit and implicit commentary upon the events of the play and these are invested with moral authority: 'I know that Marion stands in your life for your idealism . . . and that you've wounded her and it.'[61] The novel that Hank is writing is a mirror of the play itself: 'It's a fable about moral values and success', he says.[62]

The Big Knife is simple in its structure and clear in its moral intention. The exchange between Charlie and Marion early in the play expresses the essence of the play's meanings:

CHARLIE: . . . I'm Hoff Federated's biggest star. I'm worth millions to them in ice-cold profits! Hoff's got me by the tail and he won't let go and you know why!

MARION: Tell him you're leaving Hollywood for good. Promise him never to make pictures for anyone else.

CHARLIE: Just what do you expect me to do? Pick up without a backward glance – and what? Go back and act in shows?

MARION: What's wrong with shows? You started in the theatre. We'd go back to New York, yes – the theatre can still give you a reasonable living. And away from this atmosphere of flattery and deceit we might make our marriage work.[63]

The Hoff contract is a precise translation of a Faustian pact into the Hollywood environment. Success is a kind of spiritual and moral failure as Hank indicates: 'You still know that a failure is the best of American life.'[64]

The play is simple in moral structure and ends in Charlie's suicide, which is the only path left back to the abandoned self:

> HANK: He ... killed himself ... because that was the only way he could live. You don't recognize a final ... a final act of faith ... when you see one ...[65]

While it is tempting to see this play as essentially autobiographical, such a view minimises the degree to which Odets invents Hollywood as a social construct and is over-simplistic in the context of his creative vision. Of the play Odets said, 'I wanted to write a play about the moral value of success.'[66] The play is a record of the betrayal of radical heritages and artistic integrity.

Hollywood offers Odets, in short, an effective context in which to develop further his vision of mankind as isolated from the source of creative integrity, betraying essential values and corrupted, above all, by money. Commercial success correlates with moral and artistic failure. Odets creates a form of revolt in the rejection of American materialism – the pursuit of the dollar – in favour of faithfulness to a version of an essential and creative self that can transcend, as it does for the actor in *The Country Girl*, the material deprivations and emotional turmoils of life.

There is a better case for seeing *The Country Girl* as at least containing reference to Odets's experience with the Group. The interest in the play derives largely in the character of Frank Elgin, an actor who in effect overcomes domestic and drink problems because, in some underlying sense, he remains true to his art. There is, in addition, a ring of authenticity in the interaction of author, producer, director which suggests that Odets could effectively use personal experience to create the material for what is, in this context, a minor piece of work.

Odets's last produced play, *The Flowering Peach*, is of interest largely because of the manner in which it serves to redirect attention back to the earlier plays, particularly *Awake and Sing!* and *Paradise Lost*, in two ways. It recreates the biblical Noah in the shape of a Jewish family that recalls, at least in part, the Bergers in their

speech patterns and in the family tensions they represent. The play
also offers the most explicit version of fable in Odets's work. Its
interest, though, is largely historical and it exists in published form
only in a truncated version. Edward Murray's judgement that the
play is 'remarkable . . . "mature" in both form and content' is difficult
to share.[67] The text available reflects Odets's skill with varying registers: the movement from biblical to Yiddish-English language
structures is used for comic effect and Noah's rage at his frequently
rebellious sons is, in context, an effective comic device:

> NOAH: On The Holy Ark he's makin' business! Manure! With
> manure you want to begin a new world? Everybody's life he
> put in danger!
> ESTHER: Poppa's a hundred per cent right.[68]

What the play demonstrates is that Odets's gift had not, at least
in theatre, survived the conditions in which it was formed. The
early 1950s were in many respects uncongenial times for Odets. His
testimony to the Committee on Un-American Activities created a
considerable degree of uneasiness in the years that followed and,
perhaps above all, he found no topic out of which his theatre could
be built. In essence, the 1930s had given him the Depression and all
its consequences, which sustained his work well beyond the 1930s,
while Hollywood had, in the 1940s, given him another major context
in which to create drama. *The Flowering Peach* is a retrospective piece
going back to the kinds of family structure and idioms that had
been used to make the much more powerful play *Awake and Sing!*
some 20 years earlier.

The best of Odets's work can be found predominantly in the
1930s and to a degree in the 1940s, when he appeared, perhaps more
than any other American playwright, to be the figure most representative of his times which, in retrospect, are more complex and
ambiguous than they appeared to be. His considerable talent was to
encompass these complexities and express them in forms that were
passionate, articulate and, at times, profound. There are many contexts and perspectives in which Odets's work may be placed but
Arthur Miller offers in summation, perhaps the most appropriate of
views:

> He was an American Romantic, as much a Broadway guy as a
> proletarian leader, probably more so. To call him contradictory is
> to say he was very much alive and a sufferer.[69]

NOTES

1. Elmer Rice, *Minority Report: An Autobiography* (London: Heinemann, 1963) p. 343.
2. Margaret Brenman Gibson in *New York Times*, 13 June 1965, cited in Edward Murray, *Clifford Odets: The Thirties and After* (New York: Frederick Ungar, 1968) p. 113.
3. All dates cited in relation to Odets's plays are to the date of first production.
4. Leslie Fiedler, *To the Gentiles* (New York: Stein & Day, 1972) p. 128.
5. Harold Clurman, *The Fervent Years: The Story of the Group Theatre and the Thirties* (London: Dennis Dobson, 1964) pp. 150–1.
6. Arthur Miller, *Timebends: A Life* (London: Methuen, 1988) p. 228.
7. Ibid., p. 240.
8. Edward Murray, *Clifford Odets: The Thirties and After* (New York: Frederick Ungar, 1968) p. 181.
9. In an interview with Joe Hyams for the *New York Herald Tribune*, 1959, cited by R. Baird Shuman, *Clifford Odets* (New York: Twayne, 1962) p. 30.
10. *The Country Girl* (1952) was published in the UK as *Winter Journey* (London: Samuel French, 1955).
11. Joseph Wood Krutch, *The American Drama since 1918: An Informal History* (New York: George Braziller, 1957) p. 320.
12. C. W. E. Bigsby, *A Critical Introduction to Twentieth Century American Drama* (Cambridge: Cambridge University Press, 1982) vol. 1, p. 163.
13. Clifford Odets, 'How a Playwright Triumphs', in Gabriel Miller (ed.), *Critical Essays on Clifford Odets* (Boston, Mass.: G. K. Hall, 1991) p. 75.
14. Edmund Gagey, *Revolution in American Drama* (New York: Columbia University Press, 1947) p. 168.
15. Malcolm Goldstein, *The Political Stage: American Drama and Theater of the Great Depression* (New York: Oxford University Press) p. 93.
16. Harold Clurman, op. cit., pp. 103–4.
17. Clifford Odets, *Till the Day I Die*, in *Six Plays* (London: Methuen, 1987) p. 139.
18. Clifford Odets, *Awake and Sing!*, in ibid., p. 41.
19. Ibid., pp. 55–6.
20. Ibid., p. 78.
21. Ibid., p. 73.
22. Harold Clurman used the phrase in his obituary of Odets in the *New York Times*. He sees the notion as having a centrality in both Odets's work and his life:

    > His central theme was the difficulty of attaining maturity in a world where money as a token of success and status plays so dominant a role. This has very little to do with being a 'reformer'. His very flesh experienced the lure of those false gods. He struggled against their temptations all his life. (Cited by Murray, *Clifford Odets*)

23.   *Awake and Sing!*, p. 79.
24.   Ibid., p. 42.
25.   Ibid., p. 46.
26.   Ibid., p. 66.
27.   Ibid., p. 94.
28.   Ibid., p. 98.
29.   Ibid., pp. 100–1.
30.   Clifford Odets, Preface to the 1939 edition of *Six Plays*, reprinted in *Six Plays* (London: Methuen, 1987), p. vii.
31.   Bigsby, op. cit., p. 174.
32.   *Paradise Lost*, p. 193.
33.   Ibid., p. 207.
34.   Goldstein, op. cit.
35.   *Paradise Lost*, pp. 228–9.
36.   Ibid., p. 230.
37.   *Golden Boy*, in *Six Plays*, p. 316.
38.   Gabriel Miller, 'Odets and Tragedy: *Golden Boy* and *The Big Knife*', in Gabriel Miller (ed.), *Critical Essays on Clifford Odets* (Boston, Mass.: G. K. Hall, 1991) p. 173.
39.   Harold Cantor, *Clifford Odets: Playwright – Poet* (Metuchen, N.J., and London: Scarecrow Press, 1978) p. 48.
40.   The same kinds of resonances can be found in what is probably Odets's best film work in *The Sweet Smell of Success* (1957). The pursuit of wealth at the expense of morality along 'the golden ladder' in 'a dog eat dog' world leads inexorably towards disaster for the central figure. The alternative values are located in the figure of a musician. The film, co-written with Ernest Lehman and directed by Alexander Mackendrick for United Artists, has many of the characteristic concerns and structures of Odets's later work.
41.   *Paradise Lost*, p. 230.
42.   Clifford Odets, *Rocket to the Moon*, in *Six Plays*, p. 416.
43.   Ibid., p. 418.
44.   Miller, *Timebends*, p. 233.
45.   Clifford Odets, *Night Music: A Comedy in Twelve Scenes* (New York: Random House, 1940) p. 154.
46.   Ibid., p. 160.
47.   Harold Clurman, Introduction to *Night Music*, p. viii.
48.   *Night Music*, p. 180.
49.   Ibid., p. 169.
50.   Ibid., p. 155.
51.   Clurman, Introduction to *Night Music*, p. viii.
52.   Winifred L. Dusenburry, '*Night Music* and Homelessness', in Miller, *Critical Essays*, p. 220.
53.   Clifford Odets, *Clash by Night* (New York: Random House, 1942) p. 49.
54.   Ibid., p. 99.
55.   Ibid., pp. 126–7.
56.   Ibid., p. 78.
57.   Krutch, op. cit., p. 272.

58. There are several confusions about the title of this play and they derive from the fact that the first UK production of *The Country Girl* (1952) was retitled *Winter Journey* and published under that title by Samuel French in 1955. The reason for this UK change of title was that a popular musical also called *The Country Girl* was in production on the London stage in 1952. The confusion really derives, however, from the fact that Odets had used *A Winter Journey* as the working title of *The Big Knife*. For a full description of these troublesome matters, see Robert Cooperman, *Clifford Odets: An Annotated Bibliography, 1935–1989* (Westport, Conn., and London: Meckler, 1990) pp. 11–12.

59. Miller, 'Odets and Tragedy', p. 194.

60. Clifford Odets, *The Big Knife*, in *Golden Boy, Awake and Sing!, The Big Knife* (Harmondsworth, Middx: Penguin Books, 1963) p. 193.

61. *The Big Knife*, p. 248.

62. Ibid., p. 249.

63. Ibid., p. 200.

64. Ibid., p. 251.

65. Ibid., p. 272.

66. Cited in Murray, *Clifford Odets*, p. 161.

67. Ibid., p. 116.

68. Clifford Odets, *The Flowering Peach*, in Louis Kronenberger (ed.), *The Best Plays of 1954–1955* (New York and Toronto: Dodd, Maed, 1955) p. 197.

69. Miller, *Timebends*, p. 229.

4

Tennessee Williams

MARK LILLY

I start with the premise that William's work attempts to express, *inter alia*, the author's experience of sexuality and desire as a gay man who is not permitted, or does not dare, to write of the gay experience directly. We can arrive at a reading of the plays based on this premise which, nevertheless, does not purport either to invalidate other approaches or to claim comprehensiveness, but which should enlarge our understanding of the texts by exploring part of their psychological provenance. This explanation is not based on authorial intentions; in so far as these can be guessed at, they often appear confused, contradictory and, to many gay readers, actually offensive. Rather, it is based on the making of connections between the themes and metaphors of the plays and the sexuality of the writer who has created them. An example will help to make this distinction clear. Elsewhere[1] I have interpreted Laura Wingfield's lameness, and the figure of the unicorn in her glass menagerie, as metaphors for homosexuality. I have argued not that Williams has consciously done this (though of course he may have) but that readers aware of Williams's homosexuality will recognise that the metaphors do indeed bear this interpretation. (If this approach appears to be biographical, it is worth adding that works by heterosexuals can often obviously be interpreted as speaking directly to gay experience.) A gay writer, faced not only with an external censorship, but a self-censorship arising directly out of the cultural atmosphere produced by the former, may turn to an opacity of imagery and meaning which results either in a satisfying creative ambiguity or (and they are not always easy to distinguish) an artistic failure. In Williams's plays we see both.

Williams's own search for love, resulting in his usually finding sensual gratification instead, appears in the plays as a preoccupation with the male figures as sexually attractive rather than loving or lovable. Indeed, we can go further and say that their sexual desirability is largely built on their not being lovable or solicitous.

Stanley Kowalski, Brick, Val and Chance Wayne all treat the women with whom they are involved badly; they thereby become more desirable to the women within the plays. Estelle tells Serafina: 'A man that's wild is hard for a woman to hold, huh? But if he was tame – would the woman want to hold him? Huh?'[2]

Some heterosexual men and women in the audience will also be attracted by such male characters: the men because it reinforces notions of masculine dominance, the women because some of them will share Estelle's viewpoint. Some gay men will also read the male characters' behaviour as signalling a disengagement from women, and therefore from heterosexuality itself. This latter point, although it might appear far-fetched, is underscored by such details as the male camaraderie which exists between Stanley and his poker-playing friends and from which the 'womenfolk' are emphatically excluded.

Two literary / cultural traditions are involved here. The first is the idea that 'pure' male friendships are disrupted by women. European culture is saturated in the notion that ideal male platonic friendship is destroyed by the intrusion of heterosexual desire. The second tradition is that culture, refinement and kindness itself, in men, are seen as emasculating; that virility entails a kind of brutishness. Let us see how these two traditions appear in Williams.

The idea of a pure male friendship is at the heart of *Cat on a Hot Tin Roof*. Brick is no longer willing, or able, to make love to his wife because of the traumatic termination of his relationship with Skipper. (The name, of course, is suggestive of the masculine-dominated world of sport, which involves athleticism – that is, beauty – and 'healthy' male competitiveness.) Skipper kills himself when, after finally confiding on the 'phone to his friend that his love is not 'ideal' but sexual, Brick hangs up on him. (A closely similar betrayal occurs when Blanche DuBois rejects her husband after she discovers him in bed with another man, and the husband also kills himself.) In rejecting him thus, Brick has in effect killed his friend. His insistence that he is disgusted with the world, and has therefore taken to drink in order to forget, is a monstrous evasion. His father spells out the truth:

This disgust with mendacity is disgust with yourself.
You! – dug the grave of your friend and kicked him in it! – before you'd face the truth with him![3]

We can take this episode in several ways. The first is simply to make the observation, made by Brick himself, that human beings need lies and comfortable evasions. (Compare Amanda's insistence in *The Glass Menagerie* that nobody in the house must ever refer to Laura's lameness (= sexual undesirability).) The second is that these 'ideal' male friendships are seriously deficient if they crumble when one of the friends strays beyond conformist norms. The third is that Brick himself is refusing to come to terms with his own homosexuality. This last argument is simplistic; it represents a tendency amongst gay readers which, at its worst, seeks to find safety in numbers by seeing homosexuality as more widespread than is the case. It avoids the central issue: how, and under what circumstances, can men love men? That all men have a need to love other men I take for granted; that, as feminists have correctly and repeatedly pointed out, they are appallingly inept at doing so, I likewise believe. In Brick's case, what has made him take the extreme step of the treacherous betrayal of his friend is that disgust with homosexuality which the play identifies as pathological. But that fear constantly invades relationships between two heterosexual men, creating a paranoia that expressions of love between men will somehow be 'tainted' by associations of homosexuality. That this point is also clearly part of the play's meaning is illustrated by Brick's and Skipper's behaviour before the revelation on the telephone. Brick tells his father that once in a while the two friends would put a hand on a shoulder and even, when sharing a hotel room, 'we'd reach across the space between the two beds and shake hands to say goodnight'.[4] Any man, the play surely tells us, who thinks that shaking hands with another man across the space between two single beds is a daring intimacy, is emotionally incomplete.

This play, by design or not, shows that the victims of the taboo against same-sex expressions of love, verbal or physical, are heterosexual as well as homosexual. More specifically, and at the most obvious level, it also points out, in an age when very few people were 'out', the difficulty of identifying which men one could proposition. That is, we can easily imagine two gay men, in love with each other, shaking hands across the beds and afraid of going further out of fear that the other is heterosexual.

The second tradition – that of the desirability of the brutish male – is closely connected to the gay penchant for rough trade, whose essence is impersonal sex, and the fantasy of the male body as a fetishistic object rather than the housing of a person. (I should add that having created conditions in which full loving relationships between men are rendered practically impossible, leaving men in this period with outlets only in fugitive one-night stands and impersonal sex, heterosexuals then conclude that gay men are by nature promiscuous and unable to sustain stable relationships.) The tradition is best represented by Stanley Kowalski. Violent, drunken, unpredictable and insensitive, it is almost as if these characteristics are an appropriately pleasing complement to his hard musculature. He is contemptuous of Blanche's mock-modest flirtatious fishing for compliments: 'I never met a woman that didn't know if she was good-looking or not without being told, and some of them give themselves credit for more than they've got',[5] he tells her. One approach to Stanley's relationship with Blanche is that it shows Williams as misogynistic. Here is a self-deceiving, age-obsessed, semi-hysterical, mendacious, promiscuous, snobbish woman of faded gentility pretending immunity to Stanley's sexual charms. On another level, it could be seen as a healthy corrective to the male-created myth that women do not have sexual desires. Here, with a vengeance, is someone unable to come to terms with her sensuality – unable, largely because its expression has led, in her life at Laurel, to scandal and dismissal from her teaching post. She is the victim of society's disapproval – its rejection and abhorrence of female promiscuity – in the same way that Brick and Skipper are victims.

There is a further connection in the two cases. Brick betrays Skipper because of the latter's homosexuality. Blanche embarks on her life of reckless promiscuity after betraying, in a very similar way, her gay husband. He, too, like Skipper, kills himself as a result of her having rejected him.

In *Orpheus Descending*, the relationship between Val and Lady shares some similarity with the issues discussed in connection with Stanley and Blanche. Lady begins by hiring Val in her store, and emphasising, disingenuously, that she's 'not interested in your perfect functions, in fact you don't interest me no more than the air you stand in'.[6] In fact, it has already been made clear that she is excited by the casual, suggestive sensuality of his talk. Williams has mastered this sort of dialogue superbly:

LADY: . . . [*She puts the jacket on as if to explore it*] It feels warm all right.

VAL: It's warm from my body, I guess . . .

LADY: You must be a warm-blooded boy . . .

VAL: That's right . . .

LADY: Well, what in God's name are you lookin' for around here?

VAL: Work.

LADY: Boys like you don't work.

VAL: What d'you mean by boys like me?

LADY: Ones that play the guitar and go around talkin' about how warm they are . . .

VAL: That happens t'be the truth. My temperature's always a couple degrees above normal the same as a dog's, it's normal for me the same as it is for a dog, that's the truth . . .[7]

The latent eroticism of this dialogue is enriched by its humour, which is largely lacking in *Streetcar*. Far from being a mere adjunct, it gives the exchange a poignancy. When she says, 'You must be a warm-blooded boy' she is disguising her desire by means of a mild ironic mockery. In fact, she is raising the sexual heat of the exchange. Similarly, her 'Boys like you don't work' is spoken in the full knowledge that she will have to explain its meaning, which leads to her being allowed to repeat the 'warm' theme. So at the same time as raising the heat of the exchange, she is pretending to pour scorn on his representing himself to her as sexually charged. This is clearly akin to Blanche's sexual dishonesty. Both plays begin with the women trying to put down the men, only to be deeply humiliated later when the men confront the women with the latter's sexual desires. In Act II of *Orpheus*, Val is urged by Lady to tell her what he means by saying he can see through her. She insists on knowing, yet is counting on his avoiding any painful home truths – a fact made clear by her violent reaction afterwards – but actually he does not spare her:

'– A not so young and not so satisfied woman, that hired a man off the highway to do double duty without paying overtime for it. . . . I mean a store clerk days and a stud nights . . .'[8]

When Val then tries to walk out on her, all restraint and pretense vanishes:

[*She catches her breath; rushes to intercept him, spreading her arms like a crossbar over the door.*]

LADY: NO, NO, DON'T GO . . . I NEED YOU!!! TO LIVE . . . TO GO ON LIVING!!!![9]

Lady and Blanche, then, are examples of sexual dishonesty; a point emphasised in the ironic connotations of their names, which suggest decorum and purity respectively.

This sexual dishonesty is also at the root of Serafina's character in *The Rose Tattoo*. Once again, we see the struggle within the heroine's personality between elegance and refinement – the emphasis on her 'aristocratic' marriage, and (ironic?) stage directions telling us, for example, that she has 'the dignity of a baronessa'[10] – and her preoccupation with the sensuality of her marriage. As in the other plays, 'love' in its wider sense, including rapport of personality and the associated traditional moral virtues (self-denial, solicitude, and so on), is hardly suggested. Relationships – and it is as if Williams challenges us to accept the unpalatable 'truth' of this, though indeed it is a very partial sort of truth – hinge on sensuality. All other advantages are trivial or spurious.

The play's strength and weakness arise from its having, effectively, this single focus. Whereas desire is a significant part of *Orpheus*, *Streetcar* and *Menagerie*, in this play it is emphasised almost to the exclusion of anything else.

Williams's version of sensuality here, as elsewhere, is both direct and metaphorical. Directly, Serafina explains insistently and at length why, after her husband's death, she has chosen celibacy:

> When I think of men I think about my husband. My husband was a Sicilian. We had love together every night of the week, we never skipped one, from the night we was married till the night he was killed in his fruit truck on that road there![11]

There is an emotional force here, a quality of memory and tenacity in relation to it, which we are invited to respect. But the words are partly undercut by irony. The second sentence we can hear with conviction, but also as typical of a particularly risible form of stereotyping, all the more interesting as it shows a woman 'intellectually collaborating' with a set of facile sexual assumptions: the identification of passion in the male rather or much more than in the female; the idea of the hot-blooded Southerner; and the association of sexuality and crime (Sicilian equals criminal; the husband's dangerous and illegal, therefore 'virile', smuggling). Also, 'We had love' rather than 'We made love' emphasises impersonality and eroticism. (We can compare Chance's comment to Princess about the former's girlfriend: 'I was just two years older, we had each other that early.'[12]) All these features taken together suggest to some readers that Williams has simply and implausibly attached a gay sensibility to a female character in order to express those feelings and ideas which, if expressed as overtly gay, would not be acceptable.

A second feature of Serafina's attitude is an élitist one. She despises Flora and Bessie – 'good time girls' flirting sillily with 'some middle-aged men, not young, not full of young passion, but getting a pot belly on him and losing his hair and smelling of sweat and liquor'[13] – because, in contrast to them, she had 'the best': 'Not the third best and not the second best, but the *first* best, the only *best*! – So now I stay here and am satisfied now to remember . . .'[14] (Once again the strength of utterance is undercut; in this case, by the comic disorder of the grammar.) The élitism also surfaces in her insistence on the land-owning status of her husband.

When Serafina first meets Alvaro, she only begins to take an interest in him – which, in Williams, means a sexual interest – when his profile outlined against the light brings back to her with a stab the memory of the body of her husband. One of the play's messages is that Serafina's self-entombment in the supposedly ideal past is life-denying, and that to choose *second*-best – that is, Alvaro, with her husband's body but the mind and face of a clown – is a valid and wise choice. She of course does this, but only after the ideal past has been unmasked as a sham, through her discovery of her husband's adultery. Her smashing of the urn containing the husband's ashes represents her liberation from that past.

Before that liberation, Serafina is sexually and emotionally deprived, and takes it out on her daughter by means of an authoritarian attitude. Particularly, she fights an inevitably doomed battle against her daughter's developing sexual feelings and her love for the sailor Jack. (Once again, the young, beautiful and virginal sailor is a homoerotic icon available to some members of the audience.) Only when she faces the reality of her own sexual position – that the ideal marriage was not ideal, and that she can begin to live again, certainly more honestly, with a man not available for unhealthy deification – can she consent to the sexual happiness of her daughter. What is recorded in this play are the inroads made by sexual jealousy, the extraordinary force of that emotion, and its ability to produce monstrous and extreme actions. In the case of *Orpheus* and *Sweet Bird of Youth*, these actions include murder. For many, the sexual pleasure of others is unbearable, rendering them literally murderous. An understanding of this seems to me especially acute among gay writers.

I spoke of both direct and metaphorical modes of communicating Williams's ideas on sensuality. One of the play's chief metaphors is, of course, that of the rose tattoo. The phrase is a kind of oxymoron; for 'tattoo' suggests social defiance, sailors, working-class eroticism, whereas 'rose', both in its sense here of the flower, but also, more strongly, in the parallel evocation of the colour pink, is altogether softer and 'feminine'. The rose itself is of course a symbol of love and, with its dual attributes of blossom and thorns, presents both the beautiful and painful aspects of love. Williams perhaps wants to unite, in his depictions of the husband, the brute–wimp dichotomy already discussed above; the passionate, criminal Sicilian is associated with a 'feminine' colour.

But pink is not only 'feminine' but gay. Long before it had become a political colour for the gay movement, it was associated, particularly where clothes were concerned, with homosexuality. Men are still alive today who would not, for example, wear a pink shirt for this reason. The rose (as colour) motif thus combines a suggestive softer side to the brutish male, and tantalising gay associations. This ambiguity also appears in the scene in which Estelle orders a rose-coloured shirt – not only that, but to be made of silk – from Serafina:

SERAFINA [*involuntarily*]:   Che bella stoffa! – Oh, that would be wonderful stuff for a lady's blouse or for a pair of pyjamas!
ESTELLE: I want a man's shirt made with it.
SERAFINA: Silk this colour for a *man*?
ESTELLE: This man is wild like a gypsy.[15]

The gypsy analogy continues the idea of a man fundamentally strong, but sensitive and soft also; and, like Jack the sailor, with a ring in his ear.

It is not clear how this gay–feminine equivocation works. The most fatuous response, which one sometimes hears, is that these heterosexual men are 'really' gay. It is understandable that in a world full of men denying the varieties of their sexual desires in an attempt to cram themselves uncomfortably into the fixed patterns society allows, readers should interpret the slightest signs of sexual ambiguity as indicators of bisexuality or homosexuality. A more interesting response is to see the play as saying that masculinity is not, and should not be seen to be, compromised by the 'feminine'. The last play I wish to discuss is *Sweet Bird of Youth*. The hero,

Chance Wayne, shares the status of transient which we saw in Val; both men suggest, to the audience and to themselves (especially Chance), a huge gap between potential and actual achievement. Both are forced to work at menial jobs whilst dreaming of something infinitely better; as is the case with Tom Wingfield, and, indeed, the early life of the author himself.

This sense of transience is heightened by moral disengagement. Chance, as his name suggests, does not make rational inferences about his repeated failures to succeed in Hollywood; he simply does not see that he lacks ability, and is determined to try repeatedly until successful, by whatever means. These include attempting to rig a beauty contest, and acting as a gigolo. In blaming 'chance' rather than assuming personal responsibility (in this, he is a kind of anti-existentialist) he is seen as attractively free of the stifling conventions of mainstream society. Heavenly certainly sees him as passive in this sense, for in explaining his failure to 'make himself big', she says: 'The right doors wouldn't open, and so he went in the wrong ones . . .'[16] This attitude of Chance's is partly attractive because it is 'mean', thus linking Chance to the 'brute' type represented by Stanley Kowalski.

The 'meanness' is marked. Chance deserts his dying mother without keeping in touch with her during her last days; he then concludes that 'She never had any luck'[17] as though the misfortune of dying alone were an accident of fate. He gives a flippant self-exoneration when telling Princess: 'all my vices were caught from other people'.[18] The central vacuity of his life – which is the pursuit of Hollywood glamour and wealth – is turned into a significant irony, for he himself represents, to Heavenly, and even to the audience in some sense, something positive: youthful defiance, 'cool', a tempting amorality. This last quality is why he is so suitable as a companion for Princess; he has no debilitating qualms about selling his services and being entirely and ruthlessly, like her, selfish. At different times in the play, each abandons the other without flinching, when they feel that it is not in their own interests. They are both, in Princess's word, 'monsters'.[19]

So here is the opposite of that innocent, boygirl, mutually-respecting intense love seen in Jack and Rosa. Princess is paying for raw sensuality. For her, sex is the 'only one way to forget these things I don't want to remember'.[20] But even here, there is a longing for some sexual illusion. She summons Chance to her arms at the end of Act I with: 'Now get a little sweet music on the radio and come here to me and make me almost believe that we're a pair of young lovers without any shame.'[21]

The point is that Chance ought to see that Princess, the pathetic, dream-wrecked, drug-taking, lustful 'monster' is what he is becoming himself. (His drug habit is already established.) That is, he craves to enter the portals of that Hollywood where Princess is already ensconced – with hideous consequences. The gates to nowhere are those with the heaviest guards.

The sexual liaison between Chance and Princess, being mercenary, unloving and sordid, is far more real to us than the idealistic one with Heavenly. (The latter's name gives weight to this feeling.) Chance locates amorous sublimity in the past, which has all the luscious unreality of Hollywood. It can't have been (or can it?) that good, we ask ourselves. The photograph of 15-year old Heavenly provokes Chance's memory: 'This was taken with the tide coming in. The water is just beginning to lap over her body like it desired her like I did and still do and will always, always.'[22] This kind of love, whether exaggerated or not, is for Williams indispensable to genuine human fulfilment. Those not thus fulfilled wreak, therefore, a terrible vengeance, as the fate of Val and Chance illustrates (the first castrated, the other presumably severely beaten or even killed). The sexual desirability of these men is, by implication, a reproach to those who lack it:

> Princess, the great difference between people in this world is not between the rich and the poor or the good and the evil, the biggest of all differences in this world is between the ones that had or have pleasure in love and those that haven't and hadn't any pleasure in love, but just watched it with envy, sick envy. The spectators and the performers. I don't just mean ordinary pleasure or the kind you can buy, I mean great pleasure, and nothing that's happened to me or to Heavenly since can cancel out the many long nights without sleep when we gave each other such pleasure in love as very few people can look back on in their lives.[23]

In the lives of Lady, Serafina, Blanche, Val and Chance, there is a memory of, and a desperate struggle to get back to, a personal sexual idyll. The results of that attempt to return vary considerably. In Lady, the desire is chanelled into an unseemly and undignified seduction of Val, and the setting up of the confectionery, which can only, in fact, be a pale imitation of her father's orchard, which it is meant, in her mind, to replace. Serafina's ability to shed the chains of the past and accept another man – clearly Alvaro is not 'the best' – is, for all its psychological practicality, a compromise; Blanche's denial of her past in Laurel is disastrous; Val's disillusionment with 'love' leads quickly to his taking up prostitution, and Chance becomes a gigolo.

Two forces, in particular, work against them all. One is the clock. The close of *Sweet Bird of Youth* focuses on the ticking of the clock and Chance comparing time to a rat gnawing away at its own foot; caught in a trap. Once it has gnawed itself free, it is disabled from escape; the whole process becomes futile in retrospect. The second force dooming these characters is desire itself. As Williams puts it, speaking personally:

> All my life I have been haunted by the obsession that to desire a thing or to love a thing intensely is to place yourself in a vulnerable position, to be a possible, if not a probable, loser of what you most want.[24]

NOTES

1. Mark Lilly, 'Tennessee Williams: *The Glass Menagerie* and *A Streetcar Named Desire*', in Mark Lilly (ed.), *Lesbian and Gay Writing: An Anthology of Critical Essays* (London: Macmillan/Lumiere, 1990).
2. *The Rose Tattoo* (1954; Harmondsworth, Mddx: Penguin, 1983) p. 25.
3. *Cat on a Hot Tin Roof* (1956; Harmondsworth, Mddx: Penguin, 1981) p. 81.
4. Ibid., p. 79.
5. *A Streetcar Named Desire* (1959; Harmondsworth, Mddx: Penguin, 1978) p. 136.
6. *Orpheus Descending* (1955; Harmondsworth, Mddx: Penguin, 1983) p. 280.
7. Ibid., p. 273.
8. Ibid., p. 313.
9. Ibid., p. 314.
10. *The Rose Tattoo*, p. 27.
11. Ibid., p. 44.
12. *Sweet Bird of Youth* (1962; Harmondsworth, Mddx: Penguin, 1978) p. 47.
13. *The Rose Tattoo*, p. 45.
14. Ibid.

15. Ibid., p. 25.
16. *Sweet Bird of Youth*, p. 63.
17. Ibid., p. 20.
18. Ibid., p. 36.
19. Ibid., p. 41.
20. Ibid., p. 41.
21. Ibid., p. 42.
22. Ibid., p. 47.
23. Ibid., p. 48.
24. Foreword to *Sweet Bird of Youth*, p. 10.

5

Arthur Miller

CHRIS BANFIELD

Few twentieth-century dramatists have attained Arthur Miller's status. Had Miller written nothing else, his international reputation would surely have been secured by the remarkable *Death of a Salesman* (1949), which has been translated and performed across the globe. Yet his legacy embraces plays which, like statues carved in the shadow of a central monolith, focus the attention of his devotees on the recurring themes and impassioned principles of an indefatigable moral vision.

His best-known works include *All My Sons* (1947), *The Crucible* (1953), *A View from the Bridge* (1955) and *The Price* ((1968). These are plays which explore the complexities of the relationship between individual and social consciousness. Miller's characters wrestle with guilt and sacrifice along the way, their actions rooted in the volatile conjunction of social determinism and irrepressible free-will, with family structures always supplying the matrix of interaction. The ties of blood – between fathers, sons, brothers, mothers, wives – as well as providing anchorage for the protagonists to their social selves, are usefully applied as emotional tourniquets as and when needed.

It is this *force of feeling* with which Miller confronts his audiences. Robert Garland, reviewing the first night of *Death of a Salesman* in *Journal American* on 11 February 1949, conveys the sense of the play's emotional impact which left its audience stunned at the final curtain when, for 'a period somewhat shorter than it seemed an expectant silence hung over the crowded auditorium' until 'tumultuous appreciation shattered the hushed expectancy'.

Miller's audiences have continued to identify with the tragic dilemmas of Willy Loman, John Proctor, Joe Keller and Eddie Carbone. Their relevance to contemporary theatre seems likely to go on, as long as spectators continue to esteem psychologically rounded characters, and while men and women play out their illusions, desire and betray one another, remember and cannot confess, live with and act on guilt.

But there is, above all, renewal in this exposure of human frailties. The regenerative aspect of the journeys these plays take their protagonists on remains to sound an optimistic, major chord resolution to sombre, minor key development. It is this very notion of optimism, of an intrinsic faith in the capacity of change for the better, which underpins Miller's dramatic sensibility. The expression of the more moralising aspects of this sensibility together with the refusal to align with a particular political philosophy have drawn criticism from those who have difficulties in Miller's accentuating of the positive or, perhaps paradoxically, voice doubts about the appropriateness of the tragic form for the second half of the twentieth century. Yet Arthur Miller has claimed no vested interest in any one form, as the range of plays he has produced attests.

There is no single reason why Arthur Miller's popularity as playwright declined through the 1960s and 1970s. The expectation of another Pulitzer Prize-winning play to follow *Death of a Salesman* was never fulfilled. The credit with which he emerged some years after his defiant appearance at Senator McCarthy's House Committee on Un-American Activities was temporarily forfeited after a hostile reception for the 1964 play *After the Fall*. Critics found the piece a thinly veiled and untimely introspection into his failed marriage with the recently dead Marilyn Monroe and vented their wrath on the unsuspecting playwright. Perhaps as the idealistic promises of the flower-power generation failed to materialise, as faith was lost during the Nixon years in Vietnam and Watergate, and as Cold War hostility between the superpowers continued, there may have been a sense in which Arthur Miller's moral conviction was perceived as misplaced, inappropriate. No longer commanding the social currency it once enjoyed, single-minded morality had been devalued by a blurring of issues which for an earlier age must have seemed black and white.

The furniture-cluttered attic of a soon-to-be-demolished New York brownstone, where two brothers meet to settle old scores, provided a return to more familiar territory, and Broadway success, for *The Price* (1968). The play, which neatly explored the moral ambiguities of actions justified through an invention of the past, ventured into the grey areas of an American collective unconscious. Though there is no mention of the war in the play, Miller has explained that 'it was through Vietnam that I ended up there' to conduct 'an investigation of denial in the human heart'.[1]

But in spite of the success of *The Price*, future years proved less rewarding. The disappointments of the 1970s, notably *The Creation of the World and Other Business* (1972) and the subsequent musical adaptation *Up from Paradise* (1974) which used the Book of Genesis as a starting point, marked a fallow period in Miller's dramatic writing which few would now contest.

In the Eastern European setting of *The Archbishop's Ceiling* (1977), Miller attempted to create consciously theatrical resonances by having a group of writers play out their personal and political dilemmas in the doubtful privacy of an arena made public by the installation of bugging devices in a once-ostentatious palatial room. The questionable nature of truth and reality provided the play's thematic undercurrent, a preoccupation that subsequent plays would develop.

With *The American Clock* (1980) Miller crafted a ' "mural" of American society in the Depression crisis'.[2] Although the Depression's shadowy appearance had clearly haunted plays such as *Death of a Salesman* and *The Price*, it had not featured so directly in his work since *The Man Who Had All the Luck* (1944). In spite of playing to excellent houses the vaudeville epic closed a few days after opening at the Biltmore Theatre on West 47th Street. Frank Rich's *New York Times* review lambasted an extensively rewritten script and a staging which in its 'emphatic, bellowing style . . . plunges even the well-written scenes into melodrama and burlesque'.[3] Rich's comment that Moe Baum 'could have been as towering a character as Willy [Loman]' appeared to demand the replacement of one kind of play with another which had already been produced and which the playwright demonstrably had no interest in writing again.

However, in 1986 Miller attended performances in London of *The American Clock* at the National Theatre's Cottesloe to find that many of the British critics, including Michael Coveney writing in *The Financial Times*, had praised Peter Wood's production as a reaffirmation of the playwright's reputation.[4] It gave Miller ammunition to fire at what he has regarded as the paranoic commercialism of the New York stage and the tyranny of a small number of highly influential critics determining the success or failure of Broadway productions. The lack of Federal-backed arts subsidy in America has been a long-held regret on Miller's part, acknowledged over the years in compromises made to satisfy the demands of what he has called 'Frightened Theatre'. As a 'country without a theatre culture', he sees 'not that the American theater has no place for great plays but rather that it doesn't support good ones, the ground from which the extraordinary spring'.[5]

If Arthur Miller has not maintained popularity and critical interest in his native America with his plays of the 1980s, then it may be
the case that his writing has, as he puts it, been 'caught between
two theatres, the one that exists and the one that does not'.[6] It is
tempting to see this as immodestly prophetic of some future theatre
where his less-successful plays will be heralded as the unrecog-
nised triumphs they really are. But this is surely not what Miller
means. Perhaps an 'ideal', non-existent theatre has become for
Miller a kind of laboratory for metaphysical experiment, where
conventional theatre's notions of memory and time undergo
almost Döppler-effect distortion. Characters begin to disintegrate
under such conditions as the emphasis shifts from a cause-and-
effect relationship of beginning, middle and end to a non-sequential
revealing of the patterns of experience which go to make up the
mosaic.

The transition is a difficult one for an audience to make, particularly when the playwright is Arthur Miller. In the four one-act
plays of the 1980s, Miller has tried to experiment with a variety of
theatrical forms to achieve his ends, though it is also true that he
battles to overcome our expectations of his particular brand of
social realism. These later works differ in many ways from their pre-
decessors, not least in their scale.

A double-bill entitled *2 by A.M.* (later renamed *Two-Way Mirror*),
combining *Elegy for a Lady* with *Some Kind of Love Story*, received its
première at the Long Wharf Theatre in New Haven, Connecticut, in
early November 1982. Miller directed both plays in an intimate
stage setting, each a two-hander, with actors Charles Cioffi and
Christie Lahti doubling roles.

Elegy for a Lady takes place notionally in a fashionable boutique
in a New York shopping district, where a man has come to buy a
final gift for a dying lover. Any anticipation of a naturalistic style
is subverted early on. A violin plays a simple theme with a 'fine
distant fragility' accompanying the entrance of tweed-suited man
who appears as

> *Light rises behind him, gradually dawning across the stage, reveals
> [sic] aspects of what slowly turns out to be a boutique. The shop consists
> of its elements without the walls, the fragments seeming to be suspended
> in space.*[7]

The theme of the music, which Miller describes as being 'like unresolved grief' becomes an expression of the man's inner thoughts

and establishes a sombre and reflective mood, returning periodically through the piece. The shapes in the shop, becoming clearer in the light, are simultaneously the objects for the display of the wares on sale – a sweater, a garter, a watch, a cap – and the disembodied parts of the woman in mind; a bust, a thigh, an arm, a head. As the man moves into the boutique, the motionless figure of the proprietress is revealed among these fragmented forms. She turns only as he speaks.

In the move from the mundane to the metaphysical, it is not immediately clear which character creates the other. It is precisely this ambiguity which Miller wishes to exploit:

> *Elegy for a Lady* intrigued me as an attempt to write a play with multiple points of view – one for each of the characters, plus a third, that of the play – in a sense a work without the first-person angle, like the neutrality of experience itself.[8]

It is difficult to understand what is meant by 'neutrality' here. Perhaps Miller sees the multiplicity of perspectives on experience as leading ultimately to a 'cancelling out' process. The notion of an objective reality is simply the coincidence of waves of experience interacting to create a pattern of destructive interference, a flat pond.

'Do you have anything for a dying woman?' rings portentously as we are invited to allow the significance of the man's remark to sink in, watching for clues in the proprietress's reaction. The subsequent confirmation of the illness as cancer sounds the second knell, establishing this conclusively as Miller's 'play of shadows under the tree of death'.[9]

As the proprietress begins to offer suggestions and probe gently for information, the man voluntarily reveals fragments of his background. But his uncertain recollections – did he and his lover meet two or three winters ago? – are symptomatic of his current quandary: the choice of a gift which will neither mock the pain of the woman's experience nor focus on the inevitable end. To some extent we can share the frustrations of the proprietress as she tests the pessimism of the prognosis. But we find our grip on reality slipping when, as she models a silk scarf for him, she hints at her later slide into the lover's role.

Her appeal for the man to stay, with the offer of a cup of tea, is curiously comic. As he recalls a moment from the past, the proprietress now assumes the part of the lover and enacts a café table scene, throwing her head back with a 'throaty, almost vulgar laugh', and slapping her thigh like a 'hick comedian'. The transition, however, is only ever temporary, and brought to an abrupt conclusion by the kettle's whistle.

The potential interest of Miller's idea of multi-layering is often diminished by some inappropriately melodramatic interruptions, as where the proprietress is explaining her business life:

MAN: You're successful.
PROPRIETRESS: In a way. [*Confusing*] . . . I am, I guess. – Very, in fact.
MAN: But a baby would be better.
PROPRIETRESS [*A flash of resentment, but then truth*]:   Sometimes. [*She hesitates*] Often, actually.[10]

The flaw with this kind of writing is surely that, having created disintegrating and insubstantial 'shadows', it becomes problematic to invest in them the same kind of emotional depth which fully rounded psychological characters allow. Miller is specific in his directions for his actors, yet from an audience's point of view the development of character is insufficient for us to find this kind of revelation credible, or to feel that these are people who really *matter* enough to *care* about their frustrated desires.

The man's self-pity, exacerbated by his sense of ageing and the distance the conditions of his relationship with his lover have set between them, can only be consoled at the proprietress's insistence that he accepts the woman not as lover, but finally as friend. As the ambiguities return, and a question-mark hangs over the lover's future, the proprietress once again transforms to hold the man to her, pressing her body to his with 'an immense longing in it and a sense of a last embrace'.

In the man's choosing of an antique watch on a gold chain as his lover's gift, Miller pointedly symbolises a central theme of the piece, the giving of time. His representation of the time the man and his lover have shared together is suggested by the man hanging the chain around the proprietress's neck. If the moment fails to achieve the desired poignancy, perhaps it is because it is less suggestion than instruction.

The setting for the companion piece, *Some Kind of Love Story*, seems solidly in the here and now: a call-girl's bedroom somewhere in an apartment block in an American city. The clutter of discarded clothing dropped anywhere and everywhere indicates the chaos and disorder of Angela's life with Philly, her aggressive pimp husband.

Having been on the receiving end of another evening's round of domestic violence, Angela has called her sometime lover, Tom O'Toole. Tom, veteran New York cop turned private investigator, has spent five years on the case of a young Jew called Felix Epstein who he believes has been falsely imprisoned for a murder he did not commit. The tensions in the play are created by Angela's desire to elicit sexual favours from the detective and his refusal to yield to her advances while the crime he feels sure she has the answer to remains unsolved.

The dual personality of the proprietress in *Elegy for a Lady* is divided still further in Angela, whose schizophrenic manifestations come in all shapes and sizes: Leontine – foul-mouthed, gravel-voiced whore; Emily – rape-traumatized eight-year-old; Renata – 'austere, dignified' upper-class lady. Angela's fearful retreat into role is unpredictable, but handled with familiarity by O'Toole. Her paranoia seems triggered partly by his threats to leave her and partly by her conviction that the apartment is under surveillance by a police 'cruiser' parked on the street outside.

Miller's exploration of the interdependence between these two characters and the quest for a truth which might secure the innocent man's release appear to be seriously intentioned. He describes Angela as 'part whore and part challenge to [Tom's] moral commitment to justice, and of course the reviver of his moribund sexuality'.[11] Yet the melodramatic construction of the play does little to support C. W. E. Bigsby's claim that in *Some Kind of Love Story* Miller has 'forged . . . a metaphysical work of great subtlety'.[12]

For even if we acknowledge this play to be a conscious parody of B-movie detective drama, and with lines like these how dare we doubt it:

> TOM [*furiously*]:   Angela, I am just about convinced starting this minute that you are full of shit! I don't think you know a goddamned thing about this case and I am going home! Forever![13]

we have also to consider the extent to which the comic consequences of such a parody – if indeed we can find any – undermine the seriousness of the issues which Miller wishes us to address. In indulging himself in the rumble-tumble language of a Cagney gangster's speakeasy, Miller often seems to train his sub-machine gun on his own foot. Tom, the 'detective who couldn't track a diuretic elephant on a glacier' is here doubting Angela's veracity:

TOM: Kid, now listen to me and hold on tight – I am six inches from thinking that *you* were part of the frameup they laid on Felix . . .

ANGELA [*furiously*]:   How can you be such a stupid son of a bitch!

TOM: . . . And that you're still part of it right now, and trying to keep me from finding out what went down! Which would make you about the lowest cunt since Hitler! [*Pushing up his coat collar*] Take care of yourself. This time it's for good.[14]

Even as ironic parody, this kind of pointless vulgarity spreads uneasily on wafer-thin characters, trivialising the central, crime-solving motive of the detective and diminishing further any fading interest we might still have had in Angela's brutal past.

Equal contrivance is to be found in Miller's exposition, achieved via a series of laboured devices. Even if we accept the comic irony of Tom O'Toole's regurgitation (at Angela's request) of the facts of the case five years on, our credulity is stretched to its limits in swallowing his subsequent quizzing of her involvement with the affair as a totally new line of enquiry. Was he making the coffee during his six-year stint with the New York vice squad? Or are we to take this as another game-playing jest in the furtherance of a teasingly symbiotic relationship?

Miller joshes again with his Jewish telephone psychiatrist. But, apart from providing a couple of enjoyable set-pieces for the actor, Tom's *sotto voce* consultations over the phone about Angela's deteriorating mental condition only manage to crack an expositional hammer over the play's nut.

It often seems as if Miller is torn between a genuine sympathy for Angela (whom Michael Billington finds bearing 'certain superficial similarities to [Marilyn] Monroe[15]) and the irresistible urge to wisecrack:

ANGELA [*really trying not to break down in weeping*]:   After five years you don't know the first thing about this case.

TOM [*pause. He turns to her at the door*]:   . . . Jesus, the way you say that goes right down to my haemorrhoids.

The revelations of corruption in the judicial system and the framing of Abe Kaplan's nephew to protect police interests in his drug-running enterprise supply the wobbly legs of the play's denouement. As Angela prepares to spend the evening with case prosecutor and O'Toole's rival, Charley Callaghan, Tom urges her to 'bust this case' and 'walk off into that sunset' with him. She refuses, with the promise of more dubious truths about 'the whole criminal justice system' over a lunchtime rendezvous at 'Pinocchio's' restaurant. The wooden nose of *Some Kind of Love Story* gets longer by the minute.

A second collection of one-act plays entitled *Danger: Memory!* opened at Lincoln Center's Mitzi E. Newhouse Theater in New York on 8 February 1987. *I Can't Remember Anything* and *Clara* established an intriguing thematic link to Miller's extraordinary autobiography which was to be published later in the same year. The reminiscences of *Timebends* were to take the writer on a mental hitchhike ride across a seventy-year-old terrain and demonstrate the inexplicable interconnectability between past, present and future. In both plays Miller demands that characters confront painful recollections, indicating that memory can be both independently capricious *and* wilfully distorted.

I Can't Remember Anything has its setting in the 'living room-kitchen in a non-descript little wooden house, on a country back road'. Leo, an elderly bachelor, and Leonora, the widow of his best friend, have established a routine of companionship built on years of familiarity with, if not tolerance of, one another's idiosyncrasies. Their names imply that they might be two sides of the same human coin, survivors of a Depression generation which has faded like the photographs of Leo's dead friends pinned up on his wall.

The comfortable ambience which the repetition of Leonora's ritual visits has created gently coaxes the comedy out of the scene. Leo sees her as she comes in but doesn't look up from his lettering. In retaliation she helps herself, as usual, to a second pouring of Bourbon, because she has 'to see whether it's enough or too much'. Miller draws the couple convincingly and, as he proved with the ancient Jewish furniture-dealer Gregory Solomon in *The Price*, he allows the unsentimental combination of humour and pathos to work effectively in characters with a consciousness of their own mortality. Here he instils some of Solomon's qualities in Leo, whose matter-of-fact approach to his own death is counterpointed by the more squeamish Leonora's reactions to his planned organ donation.

Leo's inherited atheism and scientific certainties ('all we are is a lot of talking Nitrogen, you know') give him an optimism born of his coming to terms with the finality of death. But though he may live with his rationalism and his newspapers in the present, he shares Leonora's nostalgic remembrance of the moral crusades of the past, such as the Spanish Civil War, when 'people believed in something'. Physically, his crippling arthritis means that he is not as active as Leonora and his world is now mostly confined to the sprawling clutter of the table-top, roving from crossword to telephone sign, bread and butter to plans and back again. Checking figures for the construction of a friend's new bridge he acknowledges his mind, too, is not what it was, 'I used to be able to do these logarithms abc and now . . . it all keeps getting stuck.'

If Leo faces the future head-on, then Leonora has unfinished business with a past she cannot forget, and despair for the vileness of a present she cannot come to terms with. Her extemporary fallbacks on amnesia, as well as scotch, help her to avoid confronting the sense of loss she feels at the death of her husband Frederick, projecting instead her perceived sense of worthlessness to corroborate her lament that 'he shouldn't have died first'. She finds some solace in nature and will 'drive around countryside and look at the trees', seeming rather like her own description of them: 'they are strong and proud and they live a long time'. Leonora, frustrated by the lost opportunity of a shared life, now wishes to use her wealth generously, but inundated with so many solicitations from charities, she seeks Leo's advice in making a choice.

Though Leo has retained his communist convictions, Leonora says she 'can't remember anything political'. But, as they sit eating, with Leo irritatingly completing his crossword, she resents the impugning of her intelligence over the French pre-war president clue. Her undisguised pleasure at trouncing him over his inaccurate pronunciation of Poincaré turns the tables in her favour.

Finally, the condescension which she feels from Leo propels her towards a climactic outburst, demanding to know why after all these years he is still a 'sort of *strangeness*' to her. In an America so changed since the idealistic times of the 1930s, her frustration is in finding 'greed and mendacity and narrow-minded ignorance' while he goes on with his 'goddamned hopefulness'. It's only after Leo hints at her self-pity that she listens to his explanation:

LEO:　So if you're wondering why you're alive . . . maybe it's because you are, that's all, and that's the whole goddamn reason. Maybe you're so nervous because you keep looking for some other reason and there isn't any.

[*Pause*]

LEONORA:　It's not that, Leo.

LEO:　I know.

LEONORA:　What do you know?

LEO:　Frederick was your life, and now there's nothing.[16]

Miller establishes a sense of passing generations even in such a short piece. Leo speaks of his artisan father who 'died drunk in the entrance to a coal mine' and Leonora of her educated mother, erstwhile Headmistress of the Boston College for Women. Two representatives of the younger generation, Leonora's son Lawrence and the girl from the nature store, also feature as standard-bearers of a new age, both seeming to possess some of the traits of the elderly couple. The girl's analytical mind (she's writing a thesis on the mathematical principle of Recurrence) appeals to Leo, while Lawrence has followed a spiritual quest to Sri Lanka where he is using musical skills he has inherited from his mother.

The unexpected samba, like Leo's description of Frederick at one of Leonora's parties waving a salami and a couple of oranges at the women, is a reminder of a youthful sexuality now lost. But far from being melancholy, it becomes a joyful, albeit short-lived, celebration of a past now baton-changed to a future generation. Recurrence is, after all, to do with things happening over again.

The confrontation of loss – in *Elegy for a Lady* a dying lover, in *I Can't Remember Anything* a dead husband – continues with Albert Kroll's ordeal in the aftermath of his daughter's murder in *Clara*.

Kroll has been called by the police for identification purposes to his daughter's apartment where the murder has taken place. Lieutenant Fine, the Jewish detective impassively resolute in his aggressive interrogation of the girl's father, establishes that she worked in the rehabilitation of prisoners at a local penitentiary, and eventually manages to elicit from Kroll the name of Clara's Puerto Rican boyfriend, ex-murderer Luiz Hernandez.

The detective in pursuit of the perpetrator of the crime is reminiscent in some ways of *Some Kind of Love Story*, but the play is more engaging partly for its narrative simplicity and, to some extent, through the stylising of otherwise melodramatic effects. Where Miller had been obliged to unravel the strands of a complicated and dubious plot in sleuth O'Toole's investigation, here the focus is sustained on a forgotten name and the implications of its recollection.

Miller employs non-naturalistic devices to complement the play's ostensibly naturalistic setting. Screen-projected images over the actors' heads linger momentarily to provide a powerful visual representation of Kroll's auto-suggestion:

> *upstage in darkness an exploding flash illuminates for a subliminal instant in the air over the two men a color photo of the bloodied body of a partially stripped woman.*[17]

Here the mind and memory become the twin components of a tuned circuit, receiving and displaying stored information; in this case the horror of the sight just witnessed, and later the boyfriend's name.

Clara's appearance is not as ghost but as her father's imaginative recreation. She returns three times with a bird cage: once going off with an empty cage; once returning with a bird; then later, holding the cage up, 'waggling her finger at the bird'. The symbolism of her progressing relationship with the Puerto Rican jailbird is unambiguous. The next time she appears, Clara is dressed in the outdoor clothes she wore when, with Luiz, she had visited the Kroll's country home the previous Christmas. But her subsequent scene with her father is not a simple flashback, a playing out of their conversation one evening during their stay. It is, rather, his recollection of the nicety of the moral distinction he has always contrived to make between one kind of killing and another:

CLARA: But you've killed.
KROLL: In a war. That's a different thing.
CLARA: But you understand rage. You weren't firing from a distance or dropping bombs from a plane . . .
KROLL: But they'd jumped us, Clara. I was fast asleep in the tent and suddenly they were all over me like roaches.[18]

It is a distinction which his present circumstances ask him to re-evaluate.

Since leading a black company in the Second World War, Kroll might be said to have professed a commitment to serve the interests of socially disadvantaged ethnic groups. At any rate, as Chairman of the Zoning Board of a district of the city, his conscience will not allow him to refuse the intake of minority group families, in spite of the pressure of conservative opposition. Now Kroll's central dilemma, aside from coming to terms with the fact that his daughter is dead, is that his liberal values are being challenged by the acknowledgement that an Hispanic ex-con is Clara's murderer. Where John Proctor saved his own name by refusing to indict others who were also innocent, Albert Kroll here confronts a personal failure in uttering the identity of the guilty man.

Lieutenant Fine has no truck with the liberal sentiments Kroll expresses. In fact his twin gods of self-interest and segregationism are reassuringly upheld at the naming of a Puerto Rican killer, intensifying Kroll's sense of failure. Miller doesn't properly account for the suicide of Fine's son ('My boy was shot dead by propaganda that he had some kind of debt to pay'), but he does invite us to consider the metaphorical dead-end of the policeman's philosophy of life:

> FINE: It's greed – and that secret little tingle you get when your own kind comes out ahead. The black for the black, and the white for the white. Gentile for Gentile and the Jew for the Jew. Greed and race, Albert, and you'll never go wrong.[19]

Kroll's long concluding monologue, in the presence of the child Clara and to the accompaniment of his youthful solo of the Shenandoah chorale, cannot help but be melodramatic in its re-enactment of the 'heroic' rescue of a black company from a lynching mob in Biloxi, Mississippi. Yet the remarks Kroll makes about choosing to take command of a black company during the war:

> KROLL: Grandpa'd always had Negro people working in the nursery and, you know, I'd been around them all my life and always got along with them, and I thought maybe with them I'd have somebody to talk to, so I raised my hand.[20]

seem so curiously patronising for a man racked by a sense of guilt at the betrayal of his liberal ideals in naming his daughter's murderer Hispanic, that the ground almost begins to move from under us.

Nevertheless, Miller's intention is to demonstrate Kroll's worthiness and endorse his declared commitment to a socially progressive ideology. A past triumph becomes Albert Kroll's present justification, neutralising an individual failure with one of life's corresponding successes.

The themes which unite these four reflective plays should by now be clear. Perhaps the most significant departure for Miller is that the family structure no longer provides our principal frame of reference. Each of the one act-plays presents individuals isolated from, or experiencing the disintegration of, the social ties created by marriage or family bonding. Through ageing or loss, the struggle is now one for self-definition. The notion of the permanence and stability of relationships has been exposed for fragile myth.

Miller is still experimenting with the theatrical forms he feels appropriate for his metaphysical interests, exploiting, as ever, the possibilities for the dramatist of the live medium. If his one-act play successes in the 1980s have been limited, then perhaps it is less an indictment of the integrity of his intentions than a result of his tendency to veer towards the melodramatic in his writing, overloading fragile characters with large issues.

But in the new quest for points of reference to compass the solitary condition, Miller's characters are now confronting a precarious reality founded on the shifting sands of the human memory, and the disturbing truth that past actions may have an altered, latent significance in future recollection. It is a journey Willy Loman begins in *Death of a Salesman* and which Arthur Miller at 75 was still completing.

NOTES

1.   Arthur Miller, 'The Price of Denial' in *The Guardian* (Jan. 25th 1990) p. 26.
2.   Arthur Miller, *Timebends* (New York, Grove Press 1987), p. 586.
3.   Frank Rich, 'Play: Miller's *American Clock*' in *The New York Times* (Nov. 21st 1980) p. C3.
4.   Michael Coveney, *The Financial Times* (Aug. 7th 1986).
5.   Miller, *Timebends*, p. 589.
6.   Ibid.
7.   Arthur Miller, *Elegy for a Lady*, in *Two-Way Mirror* (London: Methuen, 1984) p. 3.
8.   Miller, *Timebends*, p. 589.

9.   Ibid. p. 590.
10.   Miller, *Elegy for a Lady*, p. 13.
11.   Miller, *Timebends*, p. 590.
12.   C. W. E. Bigsby, 'Afterword', in *Two-Way Mirror*, p. 69.
13.   Ibid., p. 44.
14.   Ibid., p. 46.
15.   Michael Billington, 'The Contours of Passion', *Guardian*, 25 Jan. 1987.
16.   Arthur Miller, 'I Can't Remember Anything', in *Danger: Memory!* (London: Methuen, 1986) p. 25.
17.   Ibid., p. 29.
18.   Ibid., p. 45.
19.   Ibid., p. 51.
20.   Ibid., p. 54.

6

Imamu Amiri Baraka

A. ROBERT LEE

If Bessie Smith had killed some white people she wouldn't have needed that music. She could have talked very straight and plain about the world. No metaphors. No grunts. No wiggles in the dark of her soul. Just straight two and two are four. Money. Power, Luxury. Like that, All of them. Crazy niggers turning their backs on sanity. When all it needs is that simple act. Murder. Just murder! Would make us all sane.[1]

So, in terms which still rarely fail to excite, Baraka* steers to a climax the play which almost single-handedly revolutionised black theatre in post-war America. The speaker is Clay, hitherto a model of black middle-class composure, who finally turns in rage upon Lula, his undulant white temptress, as they travel the subway 'in the flying underbelly of the city'. His belief that 'Murder. Just murder! Would make us all sane' bespeaks an avenging blackness, a once-and-for-all end to white tyranny. No matter that Clay will be stabbed to death by Lula, nor that the cycle of taunt and domination will begin again as this mythy train halts only to drop off his corpse and pick up its next black passenger-victim. The play had spoken the unspoken, surmised – some said urged – that only violence would truly pull down America's ancestral colour-line. Admirers saw commitment backed up by a radical force of invention. Detractors spoke of black hatred. Opposite as they may be, neither viewpoint would have denied that here was theatre to match the decade of Black Power.

Dutchman, to be sure, was not to be Baraka's only Black Power play, nor would it be the only kind of play on offer by black dramatists in the 1960s.[2] But it represents a working touchstone, a marker, for the variety of playwriting which flourished both in its own ideological mould and around and alongside it. That it aimed,

* Imamu Amiri Baraka was born LeRoi Jones.

97

as Baraka himself often enough insisted, to make America blacker, hardly surprises. For black American drama, in context, carries a double if not a more compendious set of meanings.

The first bears on the emergence, besides Baraka, of a genuinely memorable array of talent, names like Douglas Turner Ward, Ossie Davis, Lonne Elder and Ed Bullins, with Langston Hughes, Lorraine Hansberry, James Baldwin and Loften Mitchell as continuing presences.[3] The second, more obliquely, points to a decade of shifting consciousness for virtually all Americans in issues of race, in the black community a new-born militancy, and among white Americans either liberal support or an angry, threatened backlash.[4] Both 'dramas', in reality, offered mutual refractions, the one literally theatre-centred and the other that of American history itself. At the risk of no doubt too simple a formulation, the issue to hand lay in seeking to dismantle the inherited racial order and, as it were, in staging its successor.

Appropriately, therefore, it was also a time which saw the creation of a series of new black theatre companies, often actually written for and run by their own black playwright-directors. No longer could the minstrelsy and set-piece showtime which had passed as black drama on Broadway, or 'The Great White Way' as the irreverent knew it, be allowed continuing pride of place, whether with, say, the frequent revivals of musicals like DuBose and Dorothy Heyward's *Porgy and Bess* (1927) or a dismaying stage adaptation such as that of Langston Hughes's *Simple Takes A Wife* (1953) as *Simply Heavenly* (1957).[5] neither could Off-Broadway be thought to mean that duty had been done, for all its occasional productions of white-written, racially well-intended plays such as O'Neill's *The Emperor Jones* (1920) and *All God's Children Got Wings* (1924), both of which at one time starred Paul Robeson in the title roles; or of the many plays of Paul Green, notably *In Abraham's Bosom* (1924), an anatomy of early black community leadership, and *Native Son* (1941), his dramatisation with Richard Wright of the latter's classic novel of black tenement Chicago during the Depression.

First, one calls into the account the Black Arts Theatre of Harlem, and again, almost as if inevitably, Baraka, its founder and presiding energy. Established independently, in 1965 it sought Federal money under the Anti-Poverty Program for a summer community project of theatre and other cultural events in an endeavour to defuse the tensions which had led to riots all over Harlem in 1964. The Federal Buleau of Investigation, however, insisted that the enterprise had become a Black Power recruitment drive, with funds being used, among other things, to build up a gun arsenal. In no time at all, Black Arts was brought to an end. Baraka, as a result, returned to his native Newark, New Jersey, relaunching as Spirit House. But whether in Harlem or Newark, both served as issuing points for a spate of agit-prop, pamphlets, street happenings, poster and mural art, and, of immediate relevance, black nationalist drama. Within the briefest period, too, Black Arts centres had sprung up across the country, none more notable than Black Arts West, which was largely though not exclusively the creation of Ed Bullins. A leading playwright-director himself, Bullins was, also to move to Harlem, creating there the Black Theater Workshop and staging a considerable body both of his own work and that of various protégés mainly in the New Lafayette Theater.

Not all black theatre companies favoured only ideologically militant or even only black-written plays. The Negro Ensemble Company, New York-based and with Douglas Turner Ward and Lonne Elder as its leading lights, took shape in 1967, a theatre frequently given to Brechtian satire and the experimental use of fantasia and cartoon. Besides the different community and campus venues (few in the latter category more important than that of Howard University in Washington, D.C.), the list quickly extended to include Ron Milner's Spirit of Shango Theater in Detroit, Barbara Ann Teer's National Black Theater and the Free Southern theater. Production styles, as may be expected, varied. One shared resolve, however, showed itself in the endeavour to be free not only of past stereotypes of character but also of setting and plot.

The second implication of 'black American drama' bears on how these plays and companies link into, and transpose, the overall context of America in the 1960s; which is anything but to ignore by decades the familiar pitfalls of construing historical change, and within it a markedly intertextual form like theatre. Black America did not experience some simple rebirth with Kennedy's inauguration address in January 1961 (Rosa Park's refusal of segregated seating in Montgomery, Alabama, in 1955, and the subsequent economic boycott, or the Federal integration of Central High School in Little Rock, Arkansas, in 1958, might offer more likely departure points), nor did it undergo some simple decline and fall with Richard Nixon's accession to the Presidency after Lyndon Johnson in 1968 (Martin Luther King's assassination that same year in Memphis, Tennessee, would be more plausible). But even so, who looking back doubts that an era, or some very close approximation, had indeed been in the making?

Civil Rights, the Selma–Montgomery March of 1965, Long Hot Summers, SNCC (Student Non-violent Co-ordinating Committee), the Black Panthers, the Nation of Islam, the assassinations of John Kennedy (1963), Medgar Evers (1963), Malcolm X (1965) and Martin Luther King (1968), then, at a slight remove, Vietnam and Watergate: these, or a litany similar in kind, supply a shorthand, a usable contour, for the shape of black–white politics across the 1960s. Not the least of it was the incorporation of change in the language itself. 'Negro' and, as was still in use, 'Colored' became 'Black'; just as subsequently 'Black' became 'Afro-American'; and 'Afro-American', of late, 'African-American'. Alongside 'Black Power', the rallying-cries included 'Black Consciousness' and 'Black Nation Time', to be heard as much in a still largely segregated Dixie, in Mississippi or Alabama especially, as in the northern ghettos which by mid-decade had literally ignited, whether in Harlem and Washington, D.C., or Detroit and Milwaukee or Watts and Oakland. 'The definitions', as James Baldwin took to referring to them in his classic trilogy of *Notes of a Native Son* (1955), *Nobody Knows My Name* (1961) and *The Fire Next Time* (1963), undeniably had begun to change.[6]

At one end, King's Southern Christian Leadership Conference (SCLC), and the allied church groups which fed into it, in line with the older-standing National Association for the Advancement of Colored People (NAACP) and Urban League, set the standard in the South with a tactic of Gandhian non-violence and appeals to the courts, braving in the process frequent imprisonment and violence in the form of Southern sheriffs and the Ku Klux Klan. At the other end, and slightly later, SNCC and the Black Panthers, with aid from the longer-established Congress of Racial Equality (CORE), took to direct action, from sit-ins and food-programmes to (in the case of the Panthers) often deadly police shoot-outs. SNCC and the Panthers also moved events northwards into the cities. A cadre of new leadership seized the headlines, Stokely Carmichael and Rap Brown notably, alongside Panther names such as Bobby Seale, Huey Newton and the charismatic Eldridge Cleaver. Elijah Muhammad's Nation of Islam offered a yet different path, that of Black Muslim separatism and a fierce anti-white, anti-Christian theology. It too had its prize converts, Malcolm X as its missionary Black Power orator and Muhammad Ali as its warrior-king. Nor could the more amorphous counterculture be discounted; a range of dissent, youth-driven, mainly white, and ranging from hippiedom and drugs to the campus revolts and Students for a Democratic Society (SDS) and the eventual Vietnam anti-war movement. American racial phobia may not have disappeared, any more than black poverty or the disproportionate black welfare, prison and front-line army populations. But the ongoing 'historic' drama took new form when President Lyndon B. Johnson, a Texan, a Southerner, could use as his own the Civil Rights slogan 'We Shall Overcome' in a televised address to a joint session of Congress in March 1965.

Black America, furthermore, spurred the emergence of yet other hitherto subordinated groups. These embrace a first post-war feminist generation (Betty Friedan's *The Feminine Mystique* appeared in 1963), newly politicised Hispanics (the strikes of Chicano grape-pickers in California under the leadership of César Chávez began in 1965), and America's Gays (whose 'Gay is Good' slogan with its echo of 'Black is Beautiful' and self-defence movements can be dated from the uprising at the Stonewall Club in Greenwich Village in 1969). For these and yet other minorities, such as Native Americans (whose radicalisation was reflected in the National Indian Youth Council and the founding of the American Indian Movement (AIM) in 1969), 'black' had become a reference-back, a standard, by which to take on past supremacism and bigotry.

Black popular culture not only played into but frequently helped initiate this momentum for change. In everyday terms the focus could be the wearing of Afros and dashikis, or the music (and the dancing and body language which went with it) of, say, Motown, James Brown, Aretha Franklin or a young Stevie Wonder, or black 'action' movies like the *Shaft* and *Superfly* series, or the gradual appearance of black TV programmes in the vein of *Soul Train* and of black newsmen and presenters such as CBS's Ed Bradley and PBS's Tony Brown. A style of ravaging black satire, anything but 'cooning', developed in the hands of Dick Gregory, with Bill Cosby and Richard Pryor not far behind. In previously raceless malls and airports, bookshops set up special black sections. Selective borrowings from 'rap' – high-speed black spoken idiom – became widespread, especially ritual exclamations like 'Right On!' and 'Cool!' Black, or at least acting black, had become the order of the day.

But as symptomatic a 'drama' as any in black popular culture had to be the phenomenon of Muhammad Ali. To the prosaically minded, he may well have meant no more than simply another of boxing's black heavyweight champions. To African-America, however, his every punch and feint offered the vicarious satisfaction of hitting back at white America – not only by defeating Jerry Quarry and other 'Great White Hopes' but also supposed black hirelings such as Floyd Patterson and Sonny Liston. He became, and even in his decline continues to be, a conquering hero, proud, uppety, a power to revive the spirits of even the most put-upon black citizenry. In addition, he represented 'sass', a talking-back as alert as his ringwork. Further, like Malcolm, Ali would replace his derisory 'slave' name of Cassius Clay with an African one, convert from Christianity to Islam, and eventually, at the cost of his title and in the name of Black Muslim nationalism, refuse to enlist for Vietnam. Thus outside as inside the ring he became the sign of a people actually enacting the new black dispensation.[7]

As to 'high' culture, the 1960s saw the Second Black Renaissance, an even wider encompassing output of art and ideas than the Harlem Renaissance of the 1920s whose manifesto had been Alain Locke's anthology *The New Negro: An Interpretation* (1925).[8] Black fiction drew upon two crucial works, Ralph Ellison's *Invisible Man* (1952), which transforms the deeply emblematic migration of its unnamed hero from Dixie to New York into a canny modernist telling, and James Baldwin's *Go Tell It on the Mountain* (1953), which recreates a churchly and Harlem coming-of-age in the Depression. Both, it was widely agreed, signified a move on or, as Ellison said, 'around' a novel like *Native Son*.

The output which followed, another drama in itself, was to include by the end of the decade John Williams's *The Man Who Cried I Am* (1967), a compelling political-historical thriller made over from the life and exile of Richard Wright; Ishmael Reed's *The Free-lance Pallbearers* (1967) and *Yellow Back Radio Broke-down* (1969), the two novels with which he launched his virtuoso 'HooDoo' or 'black' black comedies; Toni Morrison's *The Bluest Eye* (1970) and Alice Walker's *The Third Life of Grange Copeland* (1970), each a powerfully imagined life-story in a gallery of work by leading black women writers; Ernest Gaines's *The Autobiography of Miss Jane Pittman* (1971), set in Louisiana and the fictional first-person memoir of a one-time slave who lives long enough to witness the Civil Rights era; and James Alan McPherson's *Hue and Cry* (1969), a story-collection as full of the nuance of blues and black community life as any by his contemporaries.

The impetus to black self-articulation did not stop there. New and major autobiographies came into being, few more exhilarating than *The Autobiography of Malcolm X* (1964) and Maya Angelou's *I Know Why the Caged Bird Sings* (1970). Both offered 'selves', genders, writing themselves into being, black upon white both in terms of the printed page and of the American history which previously had left blank more or less everything their lives represented. Essay and discursive writing extended the process, from Ellison's magisterial *Shadow and Act* (1964), Baldwin's urgent, bible-cadenced work, to the existential prison writing of Eldridge Cleaver's *Soul on Ice* (1968) and George Jackson's *Soledad Brother* (1970). Poetry, equally, took up its own black orientation as anthologies such as *Black Fire* (1968) gave notice, among its representative names those of Baraka, Don Lee, Etheridge Knight, Sonia Sanchez, Ted Joans, Larry Neal, Clarence Major and Nikki Giovanni. Baraka's 'Black Art', typically uncompromising in spirit, would read 'We want "Poems that kill." / Assassin poems, Poems that shoot / guns.'

For those who felt the need of it, a black cultural ideology came into being. 'The Black Aesthetic' called for hands-off by white critics and the promotion of the view that black literature should only be written according to, and judged by, in-house black criteria. The stand was uncompromising, a smack at the inherent racial (and general reactionary) biases of past criticism, not to say of past anthologies and high school and college syllabuses. 'The Black Aesthetic . . . is a corrective – a means of helping black people out of the polluted mainstream of Americanism', wrote Addison Gayle Jr, its busiest advocate. Variations were sounded by Hoyt Fuller, who would preside as editor over the transformation of *Negro Digest* into the timelier *Black World*, Larry Neal, Ron Karenga, Stephen Henderson, George Kent and the early Baraka. Black writing and art was to have its own 'black' rules of engagement, however much that prescriptivism would lead to unease and the movement's eventual undoing. Faced with the impulse of which 'the Black Aesthetic' was a symptom, and of the writing in whose service it had been proposed, black theatre could not have stood apart even had it so chosen.[9]

Baraka's *Dutchman*, to return to the dram *per se*, supplies an axis. Foremost it excoriated the American racist spiral – and any or all black accommodation of its turnings. But it also represented a triumph of stagecraft, a model two-acter whose economy and handling of pace and denouement were not to be doubted. Thus behind its resolutely contemporary scenario (what could be more so than a Manhattan-style subway?), and its warring colloquy of Clay and Lula, a far more ancient legacy of racial division could be discerned. Had not the playwright built into his piece tacit allusions to the Underground Railway, African-America's earlier Freedom Trail? Were not others to be found in slave-narratives, those of a Frederick Douglass or Harriet Jacobs, or later black story-telling with key 'subterranean' themes such as Richard Wright's 'The Man who Lived Underground' (1944) and Ralph Ellison's *Invisible Man* (whose cellar-hidden narrator announces, finally, 'The hibernation is over')? Similarly, much as Clay and Lula embody a modern couple *par excellence*, are they not also figures from biblical typology, an earth-made black Adam, hence Clay, confronting whiteness as an apple-eating bitch Eve? Of necessity, too, does not the title invoke the Flying Dutchman myth, another kind of outcastness, with Dante's *Inferno* and Dostoevsky's *Notes from Underground* as further supporting terms of reference? *Dutchman* thus enacts a Pilgrim's Progress along the modern subway ('steaming hot', 'summer on top', as the stage directions say), but also and at the same time along the infinitely darker subway of the racial psyche.

At issue is Clay's forced recognition of what he has become as a black bourgeois stalwart, his having settled for less. Lula provokes, tempts – all to bring forth Clay's dissent, her power being to enlighten and then punish for that same enlightenment. Nothing gets spared in her taunting: slavery, the electric sexual currents of racial encounter, the false coupledom of 'partying', the deeply emblematic name-calling ('Uncle Tom' and 'Uncle Thomas Woolly-Head' from her and 'You dumb bitch' and 'Tallulah Bankhead' from Clay). These exchanges, unsparing, full of ancestral charge and counter-charge, point Clay into becoming, as he recognises, an 'ex-coon', no longer part of the 'blues people' or the 'half-white trusties' (he even clubs down a white drunk). But his insight is to prove deadly. 'I've heard enough', says Lula before she stabs him, another white murder or castration. Clay's mouth, much to the point, is said to go on 'working stupidly'. As his young successor boards the train, so in default of any reversal of the status quo the circling, underground journey for black America threatens to continue in motion. Much as the vision of *Dutchman* startled, so to the attentive did its assured artistry.

Baraka's other main 1960s plays almost tirelessly extend this theatre of catharsis. His only 'raceless' piece, *The Baptism* (1964), launches into Christianity as essentially a massive sexual fetish – hidden consciously or otherwise beneath the veil of high spirituality. The Baptist Church in which the action takes place the play thus converts into a species of violent Gay Court, minister and communicants alike locked in sado-masochist rites with language to match. With *The Toilet* (1964), set uncompromisingly in a high school latrine, homosexuality again becomes a key image: one boy's love for another hidden by the laws of adolescent gang behaviour, a portrait of victimry implicitly linking sexual with racial oppression.

The Slave (1964), however, actually envisages a race-war, its principal black figure, Walker Vessels, prepared to assassinate his own children in the very house of his white ex-wife Grace and her present husband Easley. True to his name, Vessels sees himself as the vehicle of a blackness which lacking any other option becomes inescapably and brutally murderous; the same as that behind a Bigger Thomas, only this time aware and articulate. To kill his two girls, then their white professor stepfather Easley, and finally Grace herself, is to achieve a temporary, if bitter, efficacy in the face of all that hitherto has deprived him and his forerunners of self-determining power. To this end, he enters and exits from the play anachronistically as 'an old field slave', as though his incarnation as a killer were the only alternative. Easley at one point speaks reflexively of 'ritual drama', the American 'family' once more brought down by ancestral racial blight.

Four Revolutionary Plays (1969) took Baraka still further into black nationalism (two lines from his Introduction read 'i am prophesying the death of white people in this land / i am prophesying the triumph of black life in this land, and over all the world'). Each again moves in the direction of ritual, a consciously stylised 'acting-out'. *Experimental Death Unit # 1* (1964) thus envisages a black warrior group which beheads two white addicts, Loco and Duff (their half-comic 'decadence' linking them to Beckett's Estragon and Vladimir) as they compete for the favours of a black hooker. The play ends with the incantation of 'Black', an anthem or liturgy to reborn 'African' community. *A Black Mass* (1965) looks to an even more pronounced 'African' aegis by re-enacting Black Muslim myth, the creation by Jacoub, one of three islamic god-magicians, of a ravening White Beast, against which a *jihad* is demanded by the narrator. *Great Goodness of Life* (1967), 'A Coon Show', according to its sub-title, performs in its own phrase a similar 'cleansing rite', a phantasmagorical trial in which Court Royal as the old-time 'darkie' kills his own son on orders from the judiciary. Equally acerbic was *Madheart* (1967), another exposé of the delusion for black people of white orientations, this time conceived as a kind of masque or harlequin drama in which 'Black Man' and 'Black woman' recognise their mutual plight in the face of the white 'Devil Lady'.

The play his publishers would not include, to Baraka's scorn, was *Jello* (1965), his scabrous assault on the Jack Benny/Rochester comedy series. That American TV's best-known black manservant should turn unreverentially upon his employer was to challenge one of the culture's most comforting racial equations. *Jello*, in other words, sought to reinterpret the relationship as no more than a pernicious update of slavery. Perhaps, in this light, it was inevitable that Baraka would close the decade with *The Death of Malcolm X* (1969), a one-act theatrical caricature which treats the murder of the Muslim leader as a grotesquely conspired media or news event.

Other plays come into the account, notably his farce *Home on the Range* (1968), first presented at a fund-raising benefit for the Black Panthers. The piece again uses a zany black house break-in, and the riotous cross-racial party which ensues, to deride integration into the white American 'home' as a fatal wrong turning. In this, as in his other literary work, Baraka acknowledged throughout the decade that his aim had been to demythologise and exhort – though, as *Dutchman* best confirms, hardly by subordinating imagination to some one-note nationalism. Even so, the cry went up that ideology had indeed won the upper hand. The truth remains that he always managed better, in each play, whatever the risk of being charged with its own variety of racial ill-temper, a daring, even historic, metamorphosis from life to stage of the black 1960s. Little wonder that contemporaries, from the Pittsburgh dramatist August Wilson to the film-maker Spike Lee, continue to insist on Baraka as an inspiration.[10]

Alternative inheritances, however, do exist, albeit that one needs a slight step backwards in time. For in Lorraine Hansberry, James Baldwin and Loften Mitchell a more traditional liberalism was to be heard: America as necessarily bound to a shared inter-racial destiny. The accusations, thereby, however real, came over as slightly less severe, a belief in the solubility of race conflict and stereotype. In this vein Hansberry's *Raisin in the Sun* (1958), first performed in New York in 1959, understandably won plaudits as the best black play to date, a naturalist, upbeat portrait, set in Chicago's Southside, of the Younger family's hopes of betterment.

The plot hinges on an insurance cheque sent to Mama Younger and her resolve to move the family from black Chicago into a hitherto white-only neighbourhood, advance through the would-be bright promise of integration. Each Younger in turn harbours a private aspiration: Mama, herself, of an upward turn; the son, Walter Lee, working as a chauffeur and long a defeated man, of a business; his wife, Ruth, of an end to a failing marriage and subsistence living; their young boy Travis of a future; and Walter Lee's sister, Beneatha Younger, of a medical career and marriage to her African suitor. Each family member, in fact, undermines the other: Mrs Younger by her need to preside as matriarch; Walter Lee by his self-contempt; Ruth by her despair; Travis by his need to admire a failing father-figure; and Beneatha by her whimsy and sentimentalisation of Africa. Together, however, they find common resolve, a powerful self-renewal, once a scam robs Walter Lee of his investment in a liquor store and a white neighbourhood group seeks to prevent their purchase of the new house. Mama's 'I be down directly', spoken at the end of the play as they prepare to move, none the less suggests the possibility of a new dawn, a black family determined (liberally, optimistically – this was a Civil Rights age) upon a better tenancy of America.

Liberalism, too, marks out *The Sign in Sidney Brustein's Window* (1964), set in Greenwich Village and a virtual symposium on the tension of private and public morality. Sidney and Iris Brustein represent a classic Village couple, he an ineffectual dreamer-optimist, Jewish, she a 'resting' actress originally from poor white Appalachia and much taken up with Freud, and both hard-put to save their failing marriage. Around them live Alton Scales, the play's only black figure and an angry political radical who becomes embroiled in a fatal relationship with Iris's sister; Gloria Parodus, a former call-girl who commits suicide in the Brustein apartment once Alton rejects her because of her past; Mavis Parodus, Iris's respectable bourgeois sister; David Ragin, a homosexual and aspiring writer; and Wally O'Hara, Sidney's friend and Village politico who sells out to the ward bosses.

In Brustein's turnings as a man of conscience, not to say a failed restaurateur, who buys into a local newspaper, Lansberry argues for moral activism ('We shall make something strong of this sorrow', says Sidney of Gloria's death and her failed affair across the racial divide with David) and a stand against old-time fixes of political power. Thus a 'raceless' drama, essentially, it subsumes the black need for liberation within a wider humanist process, that which frees every race, gender and minority. Yet however authentic its ethic of fraternity, and certainly however well-made, *Sign* has had an ambiguous fate. Proponents liken it to the work of Arthur Miller and Tennessee Williams as a mainstay of the American liberal imagination. But to those in quest of 'black drama' dutifully particular in its attention to black culture and psychology, it continues to remain somewhere at the margin.

As far as subject-matter went, James Baldwin was to suffer no such doubt. 'We are walking in terrible darkness here, and this is one man's attempt to bear witness to the reality and the power of the light', runs his 'Notes' for *Blues for Mister Charlie* (1964). Loosely based on the Emmett Till murder in 1955, it was to be dedicated to Baldwin's friend Medgar Evers, who in 1963 also became the victim of a white racist assassination. *Blues* dramatises the life and killing of Richard Henry, a black, student-age revolutionary lately returned from a drug-recovery clinic in the North to his Deep South roots. His murderer is Lyle Britten, white store-owner and veteran good ol' boy supremacist. Two worlds thus collide, 'Whitetown' and 'Blacktown', with only occasional intermediaries such as Juanita, Richard's girl and herself an object of white vituperation, and Parnell James, the white liberal newspaper-owner, likely to steer a forward path. For against them, Baldwin leaves no doubt, persists the white Dixie of old: violent, sexually fearful, Klan-style phobia as the ordained order of things.

Few doubted the play's passion, but the cavils, both at the time and since, proliferated. Did not the dialogue dip into banality (Parnell says of his friend Britten 'He suffers – from being in the dark – ')? Was not Baldwin himself uncertain of the play's moral implications, on the one hand depicting the Reverend Meridian Henry, Richard's father, as eventually abandoning Christian non-violence by taking a gun to church under his Bible ('like the pilgrims of old', he says), and on the other hand holding on, in the Juanita–Parnell connection, to a belief in liberal salvation? What, too, of the charge of formula characterisation: Lyle Britten as sexually reinvigorated through violence or Parnell's achingly well-meant inquiry: 'What is it like to be black?' Questions, in turn, arose about the play's dramaturgy, about the Whitetown/Blacktown alternation, and possible overlength. But misgivings or not, *Blues for Mr Charlie* was not to be denied, if flawed; truly a cautionary tale from the 1960s.

Amen Corner, written as early as 1952 but not performed until

1965, drew directly upon Baldwin's own Harlem upbringing, especially his three years as a boy preacher in his stepfather's storefront church. Centred on Sister Margaret Alexander, evangelical pastor to her black congregation, it explores the call of the world (first to Luke, Margaret's jazzman husband who has returned home sick and dying after ten years on the road, and then to their son David, a music student, who rejects the sanctimony in which he has been raised) as against the call of the spirit which has led Margaret to her vocation. But the congregation's elders, jealous, full of bickering, increasingly reject Margaret, accusing her of misuse of authority and even funds, the betrayal of her vaunted churchliness. Increasingly, too, she herself comes to recognise her own complicity in her husband's drinking and desertion. The best of the play recalls *Go Tell It on the Mountain* (1953), a fervent black Bible Christianity in all its talk and spirituals, set against Harlem and the world beyond, two opposed churches of flesh and word with neither, it would seem, finally the better.

Of an age with Baldwin, Loften Mitchell entered the 1960s with perhaps his strongest work already behind him: *Land Beyond the River* (1957), the reworking of a celebrated South Carolina school-busing controversy.[11] But in *Star of the Morning: Scenes in the Life of Bert Williams* (1965) he developed a 'life' of the great vaudeville star, a documentary musical not unlike Langston Hughes's pastiche of Harlem religiosity, *Tambourines to Glory* (1963). Williams's artistry, Mitchell recognises, had to survive both racist managements and audiences bound upon seeing only 'coon' stage acts. Yet whatever the popular persona, songster or black actor self-travestyingly made to wear black-face, Williams is shown to have recognised the game he was playing. 'Every laugh at me and abuse', Mitchell has him say, 'is a nail in white America's coffin.' Thus in honouring Williams and, typically for the time, in recovering thereby yet another black cultural legacy, the play opens up to ironic scrutiny the history which set Williams his permitted limits.

Not that black literary satire could look to less than a vintage ancestry. The cakewalk in slave times offered its own mockery, black chattels outwitting their white owner-occupiers. A novel such as George Schuyler's *Black No More* (1931) parodies, from a deeply conservative standpoint, the 'race-industry' quite unsparingly. The detective fiction of Chester Himes, from *For Love of Imabelle* (1957) to *Blind Man with a Pistol* (1969), turns Harlem into a gallows-humour Vanity Fair, a stunning, surreal labyrinth. In his novel *dem*

(1967), William Melvin Kelley subjects 'dem', or white folks, to the charge of understanding next to nothing about Harlem or about black culture at large. Latterly, the 'black' black comedies of Ishmael Reed, novels from *The Free-lance Pall Bearers* (1967) to *The Terrible Threes* (1989), have taken all before them, African-America as a 'voodoo' counter world to white, official America. 1960s black drama, in turn, made its contribution, and no more so than through the three playwrights Douglas Turner Ward, Ossie Davis and Lonne Elder.

Ward's one-act *Happy Ending* (1964), 'A Satirical Fantasy', nicely sets the note, Two domestics, Vi and Ellie, who work for a white couple, the Harrisons, are thrown into near-despair by Mrs Harrison's adultery and the likelihood of a divorce. Their nephew, Junie, professes bafflement. In an age of Africa, of 'Pride–Race–Dignity' as he calls it, how can his two aunts revert to this *Gone with the Wind* mentality? Slowly, like the veteran troupers they are, they put him to rights about the real calamity at hand. His clothes, food, spare cash, even bedding, in common with that of the family at large, have come from the pair's inspired finagling; just if comic desserts for all black history's domestic service. Harrison, at their mock-solicitude, relents. Equilibrium is restored and the game resumes; nothing if not America's 'domestic' drama as a species of ongoing collusion.

Day of Absence (1968), much in the vein of William Melvin Kelley's novel *A Different Drummer* (1962), envisages a Southern town suddenly emptied of all its blacks. Work comes to a halt. Services, childcare, hospital work, cooking and cleaning, the whole support structure for white daily life, goes awry. The Mayor and Governor give way to rising panic. Radio and TV announce deadlines for a black return. Appeals to a supposed fond magnolia past are invoked. Telephones lines jam and conspiracy theories are mooted. Ward works the changes at high speed, a Feydeau or Dario Fo farce which this time mocks traditional Southern shibboleths. The Mayor, for instance, pitches his appeal in formula terms, deploring the absence of 'your cheerful, grinning, happy-go-lucky faces'. The whole, thus, works as stylised parody, a kind of adult pantomime which closes with Clem and Luke, two more good ol' boys, left to puzzle upon a vision of missing 'Nigras'. The satire exudes theatricality, but only as underwritten by a dark, accusing laughter.

Ossie Davis's *Purlie Victorious* (1962) and Lonne Elder's *Ceremonies in Dark Old Men* (1969) take alternative kinds of aim. In the

former, set in southern Georgia, Davis envisages a latterday plan-
tation with its Ol' Cap'n Cotchipee, Purlie himself as the black
minister title-figure, his son Gitlin, and a caper involving the win-
some Lutiebelle Gussie Mae Jankins to win back land on which
stands Big Bethel, a black church. Davis's good cheer, and the final
appeal to an interracial future, marks the play as written in the
early years of the Civil Rights movement. The touch is light, witty,
nothing if not companionable.

Elder's irony in *Ceremonies in Dark Old Men* comes over more
slowfootedly, a Harlem three-acter about the Parker clan, Russell B.
Parker, barbershop regular, and his equally unemployed sons Theo
and Bobby. On being evicted by Adele, the hardworking daughter,
Parker joins the Harlem De-colonization Association, an illegal
whisey operation run by a local con-man, Blue Haven. But however
entered into as an answer to one kind of oppression, the liquor
scam becomes its own monster, simply another kind of oppression.
The point gains force in the death of Bobby, killed without his
father's knowledge while stealing from a neighbourhood store. As
embodied in Parker and his sons, and as understandable as may
have been their temptation to seek any means available to escape
tenement joblessness, this Harlem adds to its own downward condition by turning predator on itself, head ironically made to bite tail.

The one further name to be added from the black 1960s inescapably has to be that of Ed Bullins, especially the collection *Five Plays*
(1969) which includes *Goin' a Buffalo*, *The Wine Time*, *A Son Come
Home*, *The Electronic Nigger* and *Clara's Old Man*. In closing with
Bullins's plays, that is not to overlook the surge of other accompanying drama: typically Wellington Mackey's *Requiem for Brother
X* (1964), which depicts the ghetto as both outward and inward
ruin; Ron Milner's *Who's Got His Own* (1965), the drama of a Detroit
family caught generationally between religion and politics; Adrienne
Kennedy's *A Rat's Mass* (1967), a piece which echoes Kafka's *The
Metamorphosis* with blacks imaged as a rodent under-class; Ben
Caldwell's *The King of Soul, or The Devil and Otis Redding* (1967), a
one-act fantasia indicting white commercial degradation of the
singer; Marvin X's *The Black Bird* (1969), an elegy to black freedom
under Muslim auspices; and Sonia Sanchez's *Sister Sion/Ji* (1969), an
early black feminist stagework. But throughout the decade, as
thereafter, Bullins's drama ranks alongside that of Baraka as setting
the standard, albeit in a style more sturdily naturalist and vernacular
than experimental.

Rightly, Bullins has been praised (by Irving Wardle) for avoiding 'self-affirming racial tracts'. His plays not only acknowledge, but seek to explore in depth, fissures and contradictions within the black community, as he has said 'the dialectical nature' of his people. *Goin' a Buffalo*, set in run-down West Adams, Los Angeles, so delineates a tense, often divided gang family: Curt as the street hardened leader, Rich his sidekick, Curt's wife Pandora, strip dancer and high-class hooker, Mamma Too Tight, white, Southern-born and a whore with an addiction under the control of the dope-dealer Shaky, and Art, a one-time penitentiary inmate with Curt. The play's title points to a dream, Buffalo as some mythicised better realm, with Curt and Pandora in their own hopes gentrified into a respectable business couple. In fact, the robbery that is meant to deliver the necessary cash goes wrong, probably a betrayal by Art, Curt's successor both with Pandora and Mamma Too Tight. But whether led by Curt or Art, this is indeed a Pandora's Box life, a black humanity forced to the criminal, brutalised edge. As the play registers the ebb and flow of the group, the violence and each temporary alliance and truce, Bullins also develops a portrait of competing styles of need, with 'Buffalo' as the fragile dream of redemption (hence the use of 'Tragifantasy' as a sub-title). The play, quite one of his most affecting, invites classic ensemble playing, a style at one with the 'theatre of cruelty' life it inscribes.

The collection's shorter plays operate in similar mode. *A Son, Come Home* amounts to an exercise in the presentation of memory, a sad, lost, mother–son relationship recaptured through a symposium of their own and related past voices. *The Electronic Nigger*, its setting a California junior college writing class, becomes the very thing it dramatises, a sardonic, reflexive exploration of the possible languages of black experience. *Clara's Ole Man: A Play of Lost Innocence*, ostensibly slum Philadelphia in the 1950s, involves an ex-GI, Jack, working his way through college, forced by his interest in Clara to confront a world none of his newly acquired academic vocabulary will account for, the lesbian menagerie which links her to Big Girl and Big Girl's retarded sister Baby Girl. It is a world which, as even tougher street figures make their entrance, leaves him bloody and literally beaten to near unconsciousness. Bullins clearly pledged himself from the outset to delineating a more diverse human order than had been customary in black theatre.

The same shows, too, in his Cliff Dawson trilogy, *In the Wine Time* (1967), *In the New England Winter* (1967) and *The Corner* (1968), each part of a ghetto tableau, an imagined black 'street' America. The first concerns Cliff's relationship with his pregnant wife Lou, their nephew Ray, and a neighbourhood which includes the one remaining white couple, the fractious Krumps, and acquaintances and relatives from The Avenue, a slightly more respectable thoroughfare. Besotted on jug wine, Cliff fantasises an escape from the ghetto through his underaged nephew's enlistment in the navy. Ray himself seeks a way out through the unnamed girl with whom he has fallen in love. But in both cases it amounts to an ironic lyricism, a doomed hopefulness. In the event the daze brought on by the drinking and the ever-present likelihood of violence ends in a knife-fight in which Cliff takes the rap for his nephew. A last would-be heroism or not, Cliff's action does nothing to lessen the black inner city as *huis clos*, a terminal condition.

Nothing in the other two plays suggests any coming alleviation. *The Corner* depicts an earlier but no less confused Cliff who allows Stella, the girl he philanders with while living with Lou, to be gang-raped in accord with male ghetto writ. In *In the New England Winter*, he emerges from jail having been left by Lou to plan an improbable ideal robbery with his half-brother Steve, yet another betrayal as Steve has been Lou's secret lover. The trilogy, if at times slightly repetitive, none the less dramatises an authentic human complexity. Cliff Dawson embodies a man caught out by racial odds but who at the same times imposes odds both on himself and others, a man endangered yet at the same time endangering. In exploring the paradox, Bullins eschews simple either/or militancy, some manichean racial opposition. Other plays written in the later part of the decade work less obliquely, at one, perhaps, with the ambitious, twenty-part '20th Century Cycle' he announced as his eventual goal and towards which he saw three subsequent collections as contributing: *The Duplex: A Black Love Fable in Four Movements* (1970), *Four Dynamite Plays* (1972) and *The Theme is Blackness* (1972).[12]

Baraka, Hansberry, Baldwin and Mitchell, Douglas Turner Ward, Bullins and their contemporaries: the 1960s bequeath a truly various, not to say momentous, body of theatre. The range embraces agit-prop, masque drama, satire, mixed-media productions, naturalism. Strengths, as guiding assumptions and language, differ. But what persists in all the plenty is an unstated consensus about black theatre as not merely reflecting change but actually intervening in the history from which it arose. Both notions of black American drama, that of the theatre and that in process within America at large, thereby fuse, shared modes of a single, continuing dynamic. Baraka in 1965 spoke of 'this aggregate of Black spirit', Ed Bullins in 1972 of 'the collective entity of Black artistic knowledge'.[13]

They, like their compeers throughout black America's most dramatic decade, were nothing if not in all senses precisely about the staging of that 'spirit' and 'knowledge'.

NOTES

1. LeRoi Jones/Amiri Baraka: *Dutchman*; originally published as *Dutchman and The Slave* (New York: Morrow, 1964).
2. Representative anthologies of Black drama include: William Couch (ed.), *New Black Playwrights: An Anthology* (Baton Rouge, La: Louisiana State University Press, 1968; republished New York: Bard Books/Avon, 1970); Ed Bullins (ed.), *New Plays from the Black Theatre* (New York: Bantam Books, 1969); C. W. E. Bigsby (ed.), *Three Negro Plays* (Harmondsworth, Middx: Penguin Books, 1969); Clayton Riley (ed.), *A Black Quartet: Four New Black Plays* (New York: Signet, 1970); Darwin T. Turner (ed.), *Black Drama in America: An Anthology* (Greenwich, Conn.: Fawcett Books 1971); Woodie King and Ron Milner (eds), *Black Drama Anthology* (New York and London: Columbia University Press, 1971; New York: Signet Books, 1971).
3. Among the more useful critical accounts should be listed: C. W. E. Bigsby, *Confrontation and Commitment: A Study of Contemporary American Drama, 1959–1966* (Columbia, Mo.: University of Missouri Press, 1968); Doris E. Abraham, *Negro Playwrights in the American Theatre, 1925–1959* (New York: Columbia University Press, 1969); C. W. E. Bigsby (ed.), *The Black American Writer*, 2 vols (Baltimore, Md: Penguin Books, 1969); Gerald Weales, *The Jumping-off Place: American Drama in the 1960s* (New York: Macmillan, 1969); George R. Adams, 'Black Militant Drama', *American Imago*, vol. 28, no. 2 (Summer 1971) pp. 107–28; Travis Bogard, Richard Moody and Walter J. Reserve, *The Revel History of Drama in English*, vol. VIII: *American Drama* (London: Methuen; New York: Barnes Noble, 1977); C. W. E. Bigsby: *The Second Black Renaissance: Essays in Black Literature* (Westport, Conn.: Greenwood Press, 1980), esp. ch. 8; C. W. E. Bigsby, *A Critical Introduction to Twentieth-century American Drama*, 3 vols (Cambridge: Cambridge University Press, 1982–85).
4. Relevant accounts of the 1960s include: Thomas R. Brooks: *Walls Come Tumbling Down, 1940–1970* (Englewood Cliffs, N.J.: Prentice-Hall, 1974); Sar A. Levitan *et al.*, *Still a Dream: The Changing Status of Blacks since 1960* (Cambridge, Mass.: Harvard University Press, 1975); August Meier and Elliot Rudwick: *Along the Color Line* (Urbana, Ill., Illinois University Press, 1976); Harvard Stitkoff: *The Struggle for Black Equality, 1954–1980* (New York: Hill & Wang, 1981); Juan Williams:

Eyes on the Prize: America's Civil Rights Years, 1954–1965 (New York: Viking Penguin, 1987).

5.   Although Hughes went on writing drama until his death in 1967, overwhelmingly he belongs to an earlier time. Accordingly, he is given only passing mention here. See, however, the following: Webster Smalley (ed.): *Five Plays by Langston Hughes* (Bloomington, Ind.: Indiana University Press, 1963); Donald C. Dickinson: *A Bio-bibliography of Langston Hughes, 1902–1967* (Hamden, Conn.: Archon Books, 1967); Therman O'Daniel (ed.): *Langston Hughes, Black Genius: A Critical Evaluation* (New York: Morrow, 1971); Arnold Rampersad: *The Life of Langston Hughes*, vol. 1: *1902–1941: I, Too, Sing America* (New York: Oxford University Press, 1986) and *The Life of Langston Hughes*, vol. 2: *I Dream a World* (New York: Oxford University Press, 1988); and, for a 'state-of-the-art' review-essay: A. Robert Lee: ' "Ask Your Mama": Langston Hughes, the Blues and Recent Afro-American Literary Studies', *Journal of American Studies*, vol. 24, no. 2 (August 1990) pp. 199–209.

6.   James Baldwin: *Notes of a Native Son* (Boston, Mass.: Beacon Press, 1963), *Nobody Knows My Name* (New York: Dial Press, 1961), and *The Fire Next Time* (New York: Dial Press, 1963). A full roster of the essays is to be found in *The Price of the Ticket: Collected Non-fiction, 1948–1985* (New York: St Martin's Press Marek, 1985).

7.   The drama continued into Ali's autobiography. See Muhammad Ali (with Richard Durham), *The Greatest: My Own Story* (New York: Random House, 1975).

8.   Alain Locke (ed.): *The New Negro: An Interpretation* (New York: A. & C. Boni, 1925).

9.   The principal contributing books to the Black Aesthetic debate include: Addison Gayle Jr (ed.), *Black Expression: Essays by and about Black Americans in the Creative Arts* (New York: Weybright & Talley, 1969); Mercer Cook and Stephen E. Henderson, *The Militant Black Writer in Africa and the United States* (Madison, Wis.: University of Wisconsin Press, 1969); LeRoi Jones / Amiri Baraka: *Raise, Race, Rays, Raze: Essays since 1965* (New York: Random House, 1971); Addison Gayle Jr (ed.): *The Black Aesthetic* (New York: Doubleday, 1971); Houston A. Baker Jr, *Black Literature in America* (New York: McGraw Hill, 1971); George Kent; *Blackness and the Adventure of Western Culture* (Chicago, Ill.: Third World Publishing, 1972); Stephen Henderson, *Understanding the New Black Poetry* (New York: Morrow, 1973); Addison Gayle Jr, *The Way of the New World: The Black Novel in America* (New York: Doubleday, 1975); Houston A. Baker Jr, *The Journey Back: Issues in Black Literature and Criticism* (Chicago, Ill.: University of Chicago Press, 1980); Houston A. Baker Jr, *Blues, Ideology, and Afro-American Literature: A Vernacular Theory* (Chicago, Ill.: University of Chicago Press, 1984). Also articles by Hoyt Fuller in *Black World* and the special issue of *Mid-Continent American Studies Journal*, vol. 11, no. 2 (Fall, 1972). For a helpful general commentary, see Marcus Cunliffe, 'Black Culture and White America', *Encounter*, vol. 34 (1970) pp. 22–35.

10.   Among the important accounts of Jones / Baraka should be listed:

Donald B. Gibson (ed.): *Five Black Writers: Essays on Wright, Ellison, Baldwin Hughes, LeRoi Jones* (New York: New York University Press, 1970); Theodore Hudson: *From LeRoi Jones to Amiri Baraka: The Literary Works* (Durham, N.C.: Duke University Press, 1973); M. Thomas Hinge, Maurice Duke and Jackson R. Bruyer (eds), *Black American Writers: Biographical Essays*, vol. 2: *Richard Wright, Ralph Ellison, James Baldwin, and Amiri Baraka* (New York: St Martin's Press, 1978); Werner Sollers, *Amiri Baraka/LeRoi Jones: The Quest for a 'Populist Modernism'* (New York: Columbia University Press, 1978); and Hettie Jones, *How I Became Hettie Jones* (New York: E. P. Dutton, 1990).

11.   Mitchell has also written his own account of African-American theatre. See Loften Mitchell, *Black Drama: The Story of the American Negro in the Theatre* (New York: Hawthorn Books, 1967).

12.   A play long attributed to Ed Bullins from the 1960s, but which he has always alleged was written by a young black dramatist who died, is Kingsley B. Bass Jr, *We Righteous Bombers* (1968), a vision of black revolution in America.

13.   LeRoi Jones, *Home: Social Essays* (New York: William Morrow, 1966) and Ed Bullins, 'Introduction', in *The Theme is Blackness: 'The Corner' and Other Plays* (New York: William Morrow, 1973).

7

Neil Simon
MICHAEL WOOLF

A characteristic of American-Jewish culture appears to be a continued necessity to revisit past experience, to return repeatedly to one
form or another of history. Hence, Jewish-American writers have
returned to Europe for myths of origin, have gone back to Depression America to confront the comfortable present with the radical
past, have gone back further still to immigrant experience to create
a sense of intimate connection between present and past, to enact
a dialogue between generations. In each sense, a need to revisit the
past, in all its fictionalised forms, seems to be an imperative for the
Jewish artist in America. In Loren Baritz's view it is that characteristic
that serves to distinguish the Jewish artist in America from his
counterpart:

> Because of America's rejection of the past, of the fierce commit-
> ment to the notion that this land will start anew, the American
> Jew is pulled apart. To be a Jew is to remember. An American
> must forget.[1]

This notion of memory is manifest in many forms. Charles
Reznikoff's *Family Chronicle* (1963) is an act of domestic reconciliation in which the son gathers the memoirs of mother and father to
create an enacted dialogue between generations. A retrospective
sense of mutual understanding links mother and son, and Sarah
Reznikoff's chronicle contains within it the precise reason why there
is an imperative to carry the past into the future:

> One day, one of our cousins who had just arrived from Russia,
> was in our house; and when it was nearly three o'clock, all the
> children came running out of school – so many of them – and his
> eyes filled with tears. I remembered how I, too, had longed for an
> education. 'We are a lost generation,' I said. 'It is for our children
> to do what they can.'[2]

117

A burden of sacrifice cannot easily be cast aside and past suffering is manifestly a presence in the comfortable present encapsulated in memory or, in Philip Roth's novella *Goodbye Columbus* (1959), in material objects retained in the attic like talismans from the impoverished past:

> Brenda went into the room. When the puny sixty-watt bulb was twisted on, I saw that the place was full of old furniture – two wing chairs with hair-oil lines at the back, a sofa with a paunch in its middle, a bridge table, two bridge chairs with their stuffing showing, a mirror whose backing had peeled off, shadeless lamps, lampless shades, a coffee table with a cracked glass top, and a pile of rolled up shades.
> 'What is this?' I said.
> 'A storeroom. Our old furniture.'
> 'How old?'
> 'From Newark,' she said.[3]

There is something within what Alfred Kazin calls 'the radical confidence of the 1930s'[4] that persistently calls to the imagination of Jewish-American writers. Malamud is driven to reinvent the 1930s in *The Assistant*. Henry Roth's neglected novel of 1934, *Call It Sleep* begins to assume some kind of centrality in Jewish-American culture. All of this appears to enact Daniel Bell's notion that 'to be a Jew is to be part of a community woven by memory'.[5] However, this memory is not always or inevitably expressed with Malamud-like solemnity or with the radical commitment of Clifford Odets. A most extreme example of the presentation of the 1930s as comedy is found in Wallace Markfield's blackly humorous *Teitelbaum's Window* (1970). A group of 1930s radicals, for example, enlist the views of the black maid Lurinea:

> Herewith Mr Sobler pointed out that these sorrows, these burdens, the burden of these sorrows would one day surely pass, and he hoped that he had contributed in a fashion and in a small way to to easing with that pamphlet, now Lurinea's to keep, dramatizing, dealing with, dramatically dealing with the Scottsboro Boys.
> Forthrightly, Lurinea made her views known, answering, 'Morgan, droogan droogan, droogan droogan morgan, droogan,'

then with the kindest of smiles and a courteous and dignified, 'Morgan,' retired to the foyer.

Immediately, Mrs Sobler followed hastening to help with Lurinea's coat, responding to her 'Droogan morgan' by a barely audible, 'Yes but Thursday isn't so good for *us*.'[6]

The past then, in all its forms, is a particularly potent landscape for the Jewish writer in America and there are many strategies for exploring that past from high seriousness to comedy. Much of Neil Simon's work can be seen within this kind of perspective, as representing in one form or another a persistent re-examination of the past, sometimes directly as in *Brighton Beach Memoirs* or indirectly, through the consciousness of characters, in *The Prisoner of Second Avenue* or *The Sunshine Boys*. Characteristic of Simon's engagement with the past is that history is seen consistently through the lens of nostalgia. Nostalgia is history edited by sentiment and Simon projects a view of the past as, inevitably, a richer landscape than that of the present. In that, above all, is his popularity. He looks back upon the past through softening lenses, makes of it, and its anxieties, a world, if not rose-coloured, at least profoundly softened. Softening the cutting edges of suffering is a primary mode for Jewish sentimental literature from Potash and Permutter through Harry Golden and, in a direct line to Neil Simon, in the Yiddish Theatre in its non-realist, non-political mode. A central strategy in this process of editing the past is in the use of a domestic structure in which past suffering can be perceived, contained and ameliorated.

This process is most clearly exemplified in *Brighton Beach Memoirs* (1982). The play is set in 1937 and it makes frequent reference to the traumas of Jewish experience in Europe and, of course, sufferings associated with economic depression within the USA, the increasing tension in Europe associated with the rise of Hitler and so on. The experiences are, however, filtered through and narrated by the 15-year-old Eugene and his is the controlling perception of the play which directly offers a commentary on events to the audience. The perspective is a relatively innocent one and it is unchallenged by any other coherent perception. Only the audience's knowledge of historical reality can be brought to bear to place this youthful perception in context. Simon's Eugene is a clearly autobiographical figure but his real function in the play is, in a sense, to obliterate and obscure suffering. What the play finally proposes is the restorative power of family love. It demonstrates how love transcends tension and suffering. It is what persists in memory. Such a process of transformation is signalled in Simon's dedication at the beginning of the published version:

> To my parents, grandparents, brother, cousins, aunts, uncles, and especially to those who endured the pains, insecurities, fears, joys, love and fellowship of New York City in the Depression Years.[7]

Other writers have, of course, used childhood perception as the controlling mode through which to revisit suffering. L. P. Hartley's *The Go-between* or even Salinger's *Catcher in the Rye* have employed related strategies but the novel form permits other perceptions space in which to contextualise the child's perception. The problem in *Brighton Beach Memoirs* is that Eugene is both the most innocent and the brightest figure in the play. There is no real challenge to his perception of events except, of course, the audience's sense of history. The ultimately wholesome nature of the family life represented thus contains and ameliorates domestic anguish, and Eugene's presumably painful rite of passage from childhood to adulthood.

Throughout the play Eugene repeatedly directly addresses the audience and offers commentary on domestic upheavals as they occur. His commentary is both a comic counterpoint and a means, often through bathos, of undermining whatever felt anguish is generated. Thus, the possible loss of Stan's job, a serious matter to the marginal economy in the Morton family in 1937, evokes this response: 'Oh, God! As if things weren't bad enough . . . and now this! The ultimate tragedy . . . liver and cabbage for dinner! A Jewish medieval torture!' (p. 29). A sequence of tensions evoke the emotional landscape of Arthur Miller's *Death of a Salesman* but Eugene's voice is consistently used to direct the emotional response of the audience away from those tensions. The action of the play contains the political and domestic unease within a structure that serves to limit destructiveness.

A crucial scene shows a potential confrontation between Jack, Eugene's father, and Stan, his older brother, after it is discovered that Stan has lost all his wages gambling. Fathers and sons, a rich landscape of confrontation in Jewish-American writing, become reconciled through love. Jack's anger evaporates because of, among other things, consciousness of the wider conflict: 'There's going to be a war. A terrible war, Stanley' (p. 122) and, above all, because of the transcending power of familial love:

Don't you know, Stanley, there's nothing you could ever do that was so terrible, I couldn't forgive you. I know why you gambled. I know how terrible you feel. It was foolish, you know that already. I've lost money gambling in my time. I know what it's like.   (p. 124)

Throughout Jewish-American writing the tension and ambiguities of father–son relationships are used to reflect the reality of generational separation. In the immigrant experience, for example, the father often represented continuity with European forms and religious/social practices that were discarded by the 'Americanised' son. Father–son relationships were frequently used to express the division of generations that came to be seen as an inevitable consequence of American-Jewish experience. That kind of tension is expressed by Alfred Kazin in his perspective on 1960s radicalism:

> The young en masse suddenly became revolutionaries against all fixed things. They were terrible, outrageous; they were outside of literature, they were even anti-literature. But since they were our children, children of the new middle class, they were perfectly equipped and ready to dynamite us.
>
> The sons were out to get the fathers – especially if the fathers had been 'radicals' during a certain ancient Depression.[8]

Simon uses Jack and Stanley to bridge the kind of divide that permeates Jewish-American writing. Where other artists, like Miller in *Death of a Salesman*, have exploited the dramatic potential of conflict, Simon uses the sentimental potential contained within the resolution of conflict.

The power of family love, another pervasive Jewish theme, triumphs over conflict in Simon's dramatic system, as in the reverse (mother–daughter) situation in *The Gingerbread Lady*. Evy is a semi-reformed alcoholic who is aided by the wisdom of Polly her daughter. Mother and daughter roles are reversed as Polly acts as a force for resolution and wholeness against conflict and disintegration. Role-reversal is fully enacted in the end of the play where Polly moves toward establishing some kind of a domestic resolution. The play ends with her mother's assertion that 'When I grow up, I want to be just like you'.[9] Simon's dramatic landscape serves to reunite the generations across the emotional divides that have given many of his contemporaries their creative environments.

Thus, Neil Simon in this area represents some kind of shaman to at least one of his potential audiences: an urban middle-class, middle-aged Broadway theatre-going group. One function of Broadway theatre has been to offer images of comfort, in the end not to disturb, or at least not to disturb too badly or permanently. The prevailing mood of resolution, be it through comedy and/or through nostalgic editing of history, serves that audience particularly well and also translates particularly well into Hollywood. More than any other popular writer of his period, Simon has with ease functioned successfully in several media: initially in television as a writer for Phil Silvers and Sid Caesar, then on Broadway both through plays and musicals, and in movies. Simon's wit is, of course, a key factor in that popularity but beneath that is the sense of reconciliation that he brings to his audience. He raises anxieties that reverberate around the culture and times experienced by his audience but then these anxieties are dispersed, resolved.

This is most clearly expressed in Eugene's closing exhortation in *Brighton Beach Memoirs*. News of Jack's relatives' escape from Poland coincides with Eugene's discovery of the naked female form. In an ending that is profoundly bathetic, and in a manner that parodies the ending of Clifford Odets's *Awake and Sing!* (1935), Eugene projects a future: 'A momentous moment in the life of I, Eugene Morris Jerome. I have seen the Golden Palace of the Himalayas . . . Puberty is over. Onwards and upwards!' (p. 130). The contrast with Odets offers an insight into Simon's ideology, such as it is. Odets uses Ralph to project a continued struggle; experience has led to a sense of renewed commitment:

> My days won't be for nothing. Let Mom have the dough. I'm twenty-two and I'm kicking! I'll get along. Did Jake die for us to fight about nickels? No! 'Awake and sing', he said. Right here he stood and said it. The night he died, I saw it like a thunderbolt! I saw he was dead and I was born! I swear to God, I'm one week old![10]

The contrast between the two plays is revealing in other senses. *Awake and Sing!* was written in 1935 and occupies some of the same sociological ground. As Odets tells the reader, his characters 'share a fundamental activity: a struggle for life amidst petty conditions'.[1] In that respect they occupy exactly the same space as the Mortons. However, Ralph's exhortation to 'Awake and sing!' reflects a process of learning in which difficult experience has been transformed into action and has, in turn, had a transforming effect on the character ('born-again' into political consciousness). In contrast, Eugene is relatively untouched by experience despite his own sense of passing from childhood to manhood through suffering:

> I guess there comes a time in everybody's life when you say, 'This very moment is the end of my childhood.' When Stanley closed the door, I knew that moment had come to me . . . I was scared. I was lonely . . . If it was suffering I was after, I was beginning to learn about it. (p. 108)

That said, experience makes no felt impact on Eugene in the play. The voice that opens the play is consistent with that which closes it. If Odets's ideology is ultimately a simple one, it reflects a version of experience as directional, leading toward some form of enlightenment, as Eric Mottram recognises in his discussion of the impact of the patriarchal Jacob on Ralph: 'He hands on to his grandson, Ralph, not Communist dogma but a healthful urge towards change and a hope for a developed life.'[12] In contrast, 'onwards and upwards' is a comic sexual innuendo that reflects an unlearned experience, that serves to enforce Simon's version of the past as edited, as containing a sense of pain without integrating that pain either into the dynamics of the play or into the consciousness of the characters.

Nostalgia for an idealised past is a seductive emotion. It appeals to popular conservatism and to the sense that things were somehow better, that despite notions to the contrary the world has not progressed but regressed from some state of perfection. This is in essence an Edenic notion that, when personalised, drives the emotions back towards childhood for images with which to confront the uneasy present.

Simon's use of sport as a location of childhood simplicity in *Brighton Beach Memoirs* and elsewhere is both characteristically an American device and common to other, more sophisticated, voices such as Philip Roth's. In *Portnoy's Complaint*, the protagonist hopelessly yearns for his own childhood in terms of a simple moral universe to be found in the baseball diamond: 'Oh, to be a center fielder, a center fielder – and nothing more.'[13] The same kind of impulse can be found in W. P. Kinsella's *Shoeless Joe* (1982) and in many other forms, not least in Malamud's *The Natural*. Both

Kinsella's novel and the movie version *Field of Dreams* project a world where simplicities are reclaimed, and a location that is alternative to the disturbing actualities of the adult present. Shoeless Joe recalls the attractions of baseball in a manner that locates them within the lost world of childhood:

> I loved the game . . . I'd have played for food money. I'd have played free and worked for food. It was the game, the parks, the smells, the sounds. Have you ever held a bat or a baseball to your face? The varnish, the leather. And it was the crowd, the excitement of them rising as one when the ball was hit deep . . . It makes me tingle all over *like a kid* on his way to his first double-header, just to talk about it.[14]

For Simon, sport is a means of negating complex realities and is, in a sense, a temporary pathway back to the simplicities of youth. That is exactly the spirit of the poker ritual in *The Odd Couple*: a means of holding at bay adult (and female) realities through simplifying (and masculine) rituals. Even in probably the bleakest of Simon's plays, *The Prisoner of Second Avenue*, sport offers the beleaguered Mel some kind of fantasy of escape from urban adult reality.

The Prisoner of Second Avenue is not only Simon's bleakest play; it is in many respects his best and it certainly exemplifies many of the themes that run through his work. In this discussion of the play, some of the essential preoccupations of Simon's work are focused. Urban anxiety is both real and countered through the wisecrack and through nostalgia. Underlying the play is a sense of masculine loss in an environment characterised by angst, alienation, over-competitiveness and hostility. Alternative dreamed locations are envisaged and discarded and they are drawn both from childhood and from classical American myth landscapes of innocence: the open world of nature and space, the dreamed and lost frontier of the American imagination. If these are characteristic Simon themes they are characteristically contained by Simon's sense of comedy and by a profound sense of nostalgia for the lost world of childhood:

> MEL: Food used to be so good. I used to love food. I haven't eaten food since I was thirteen years old.
>
> EDNA: Do you want some food? I'll make you food. I remember how they made it.

MEL: I haven't had a real piece of bread in thirty years. If I knew
what was going to happen, I would have saved some rolls
when I was a kid.[15]

A mordant and bathetic comic voice drawn out of Jewish, New
York humour does not obscure a sense of present loss contrasted
with past richness.

At the heart of *The Prisoner of Second Avenue* is a sense of the
fragility of urban security and its illusory nature. On the prosper-
ous Upper East Side of Manhattan, Mel and Edna Edison are beset
by a sequence of natural and unnatural disasters that serve to em-
phasise a version of urban reality as profoundly alienating, meta-
phorically imprisoning the Edison's. They are, of course, ironically
named. Progressively urban experience conspires to 'darken' their
landscapes. The 'usual' hazards of urban life, cramped living conditions, noisy neighbours and so on, gradually give way to an
accumulation of disasters that suggest some kind of cosmic, and
comic, conspiracy. In this respect, Simon's landscape exactly cor-
responds to that of another of Sid Caesar's scriptwriters, Woody
Allen: 'Even the cactus is dying. Strongest plant in the world, only
has to be watered twice a year. Can't make a go of it on Eighty-
eighth and Second' (p. 251). Simon uses two dramatic devices to
enforce this view of the hostility of urban experience. In the first,
the Edisons are subject to a sequence of events including lost jobs,
robbery, aggressive neighbours, breakdowns and so on, that conspire
to make their lives literally unbearable. The other device is the voice
of the newsreader that punctuates the play at various points. The
combined effect is to present the city as an irrational landscape and
the experience of the Edisons as more than personal misfortune.
They are victims of a world close to a kind of absurd disintegration:

This is the *Six O'Clock Report* with Stan Jennings sitting in for Roger
Keating, who was beaten and mugged last night outside our stu-
dio following the *Six O'Clock Report* . . . A Polish freighter, the six-
thousand-ton *Majorska*, sailed into New York harbor in dense fog
at 7:00 A.M. this morning and crashed into the Statue of Liberty.
Two seamen were injured and electrical damage caused flickering
in Miss Liberty's torch. . . .
. . . And today, in a midtown hotel following a convention
of the national Psychiatric Society, seventeen of the leading

psychiatrists in the United States were trapped between floors in
an elevator for over forty-five minutes. Panic broke out and twelve
of the doctors were treated for hysteria.   (p. 309)

Against such a world, a sequence of failed defences are established. The first are fairly typical and familiar Jewish-comic devices
such as bathos and hyperbole. In essence, what Simon frequently
proposes is an ancient solution to suffering: what cannot be cured
must be endured. In this play, however, that stoicism disintegrates
and there are several moments of retreat that end in a failure to
escape. Edna proposes one archetypal American solution:

EDNA: We don't have to live in the city. We could move somewhere in the country, or even out west.
MEL: And what do I do for a living? Become a middle-aged cow-
boy? Maybe they'll put me in charge of rounding up the elderly cattle. . . .   (p. 252)

Mel's response to this and Edna's other alternatives reveals the
degree to which the metaphorical prison of the title becomes real.
Dreams of Europe, of escape to Vermont, of starting a holiday camp
for children are progressively revealed as fragile and futile. The
path that Simon plots is uncharacteristically bleak and unresolved.
Mel has a breakdown which leads to a sense of paranoia and notions of conspiracy:

There *is* a plot Edna. It's very complicated, very sophisticated,
almost invisible . . . Maybe only a half a dozen people in this
country really know about.   (p. 284)

The stasis at the end of the play ('a contemporary American Gothic';
p. 320) is unresolved and the situation remains in suspension. In
that respect, this play brings Simon much closer to his contemporaries in a view of contemporary reality as fundamentally hostile
and irrational. The metaphor of urban experience as a kind of prison
is not, of course, an unfamiliar one but it serves to bring the play
into an area of shared analysis with those darker voices of contemporary culture, exemplified by Philip Roth's view of the cultural
environment: 'It stupefies, it sickens, it infuriates, and finally it is
even a kind of embarrassment to one's own meager imagination.'[16]
Underlying this play is a critique of American materialism and

an expression of the failure of prosperity. It recalls, in that respect, Saul Bellow's view of prosperity as a kind of 'swamp':

> For in the past what could money buy that can compare with the houses, the sinks, the garbage disposals, the Jags, the minks, the plastic surgery. . . . To what can we compare this change? Nothing like it has ever hit the world; nothing in history has so quickly and radically transformed any group of Jews.[17]

Simon explores a recurrent theme in post-war American culture: the notion that material success is a kind of moral failure, that American urban life has failed to create a quality of life that is sustainable and desirable.

If that were the whole issue in the play, it would be difficult to see the play within the mainstream of Simon's work, but that is not in fact the case. Simon's use of humour and self-deprecation is as attractive as ever to his potential audience. The play also contains a somewhat more subtle, and attractive, message to the Broadway audience. The Edisons are victims of circumstances largely beyond their control but they are also, by implication unlike the audience, failed survivors of the urban experience. As Edna says, 'You either live with it or you get out' (p. 249). The play speaks to the survivor mentality of urban New York and, in that respect, its popularity is enforced by the bleak portrait of contemporary life that it sustains.

The other central concern in Simon's work, not unrelated to urban disorder, is the presentation of sexual relations in post-Kinsey America. This might most clearly be seen by contrasting *The Odd Couple* (1966) with *Chapter Two* (1978). In both plays, divorce is a major fact of the network of relationships. The relationships between the sexes is characterised by both conflict and need. These models are contrasted with mutually supportive relationships within the sexual groups. Thus, the regular poker game in *The Odd Couple* is seen as an all-male oasis in the complex world, a moment of calm in which the pressures of female reality (divorce, sexual need, romance, alimony) are replaced by a simpler world related, as discussed earlier, to the simplifications of sport. Similarly, in *Chapter Two* the relationships between Faye and Jennie and between George and Leo are supportive and strong whereas the developing complications among the couples suggest relationships teetering on the edge of disintegration but persistent in their emotional imperatives. The disorder of sexual relationships, the frailty of marriage and love, are symptoms of the wider kinds of disorder discussed earlier but they also offers a broad comic canvas exploited fully by Simon in the episodic plays such as *California Suite*. In this area, Simon's work teeters frequently on the edge of farce and, indeed, goes over that edge in *Rumors*.

To see Simon primarily as a dramatist of sexual confusion is not though, in then end, the most interesting perspective on his work and its significance within contemporary American culture. Simon justly engages our attention for a number of reasons. In the first case, he popularises a perception of contemporary urban life as simultaneously profoundly hostile and comic: a view that is represented within other contemporary cultural forms and that typifies the current conception of New York City as some kind of exemplifier of city chaos – a 'concrete' manifestation of a contemporary malaise. Simon's language also typifies what is perceived as New York speech in that it combines mordant irony with elements of sentimentality. Essentially, Simon has both recreated, and invented, an instantly identifiable dramatic language that is well-suited to carry a combination of anxiety, neurosis and wit.

Simon also has a place in the cultural history of Jewish America. In one sense, there is a direct line between him and those Hollywood pioneers who translated Jewish nostalgia into a universally popular art form characterised, at least in part, by sentimentality. In *An Empire of Their Own*, Neil Gabler summarises the legacy of the early Jewish pioneers in Hollywood:

> what the Hollywood Jews left behind is something powerful and mysterious. What remains is a spell, a landscape of the mind, a constellation of values, attitudes, and images, a history and a mythology that is part of our culture and our consciousness.[18]

Simon has worked, in his generation, models of Jewish experience and language with forms which have had for over 30 years a considerable popular success. In that respect, he has built on the legacy of the Hollywood Jews using some of their strategies and, in part, the medium they created.

An essential characteristic of Simon's work is an engagement with the past: a recurrent need to reperceive the present through the filter of versions of history. George's assertion in *Chapter Two* that 'You can't get to the present without going through the past'[19] expresses precisely an impulse that places many of the plays within a tradition of Jewish writing in America, within also a tradition of Jewish consciousness that has shaped Simon's subject matter. There is, in secular America, a version of Jewish experience that is reliant neither on God nor on religious practice. It is a state of mind in which the past contains moral imperatives which compel the artist to express, in some form or another, a line of continuity between the comfortable present and the darker past. Simon's work also belongs, at least in part, somewhere on that line of continuity.

Finally, whatever critical judgement may be placed on the plays, the seriousness of Simon's intention is not in dispute. Almost without exception, Simon's plays confront in one form or another realities of contemporary experience. Comedies of urban disorder seem as good a way of characterising his work as a whole. To those who live in the great metropolises of the West, to those who endure the disorders of urban life, to those who perceive comedy at the edge of dissolution, Neil Simon has something to say about experience. He, certainly, has never been in any doubt about the essential seriousness of his art:

> Humor isn't anything if it can't make you think and feel. Anyone can make a baby laugh by shaking a rattle in its face. I don't want to write for infants and shake rattles.[20]

NOTES

1. Loren Baritz, 'A Jew's American Dilemma', *Commentary*, vol. 33, no. 6 (June 1962) p. 525.
2. Sarah Reznikoff, 'Early History of a Seamstress', in Charles Reznikoff, *Family Chronicle* (London: Norton Bailey, 1969) p. 99.
3. Philip Roth, *Goodbye Columbus, and Five Short Stories* (Boston, Mass.: Hougton Mifflin, 1989) p. 67.
4. Alfred Kazin, *New York Jew* (London: Secker & Warburg, 1978) p. 4.
5. Daniel Bell, 'Reflections on Jewish Identity', *Commentary*, vol. 31, no. 6 (June 1961) p. 474.
6. Wallace Markfield, *Teitelbaum's Window* (London: Jonathan Cape, 1971) pp. 254–5.
7. Neil Simon, *Brighton Beach Memoirs* (New York: Random House, 1984), unnumbered frontispiece. All further references are to this edition and are placed within the text.
8. Kazin, *New York Jew*, pp. 258–9.
9. Neil Simon, *The Gingerbread Lady*, in *The Collected Plays of Neil Simon*, vol. 2 (New York: Random House, 1979) p. 238.

10.   Clifford Odets, *Awake and Sing!*, in *Golden Boy, and Other Plays* (Harmondsworth, Middx: Penguin, 1963) pp. 182–3.
11.   Ibid., p. 117.
12.   Eric Mottram, 'Introduction' to Odets, *Golden Boy and Other Plays*, p. 13.
13.   Philip Roth, *Portnoy's Complaint* (London: Jonathan Cape, 1969) p. 72.
14.   W. P. Kinsella, *Shoeless Joe* (New York: Ballantine Books, 1989) p. 13. My emphasis.
15.   Neil Simon, *The Prisoner of Second Avenue*, in *The Collected Plays*, vol. 2, p. 248. All further references are to this edition and are placed in the text.
16.   Philip Roth, 'Writing American Fiction', in *Reading Myself and Others* (London: Jonathan Cape, 1975) p. 120.
17.   Saul Bellow, 'The Swamp of Posterity', *Commentary*, vol. 28, no. 4 (July 1959) pp. 78–9.
18.   Neil Gabler, *An Empire of Their Own: How the Jews Invented Hollywood* (New York: Doubleday, 1988) p. 432.
19.   Neil Simon, *Chapter Two*, in *The Collected Plays*, vol. 2, p. 745.
20.   Quoted in William and Rhoda Cahn, *The Great American Comedy Scene* (New York: Monarch, 1978) p. 156.

8

Sam Shepard

MICHAEL J. HAYES

Wherever you look in Sam Shepard's work people are trying to make it. Whether it's on the ranch, at the rodeo, on the road or in the exploding intimacy of family relationships, people are trying to survive. And there aren't any sanctioned rules. People are trying to do the best they can with what they have within themselves, within their heredity and from their experience of life.

Shepard was born in 1943 just when America was being forced out of its isolation by the ruling elite and by Pearl Harbor. The 1960s started when Sam Shepard was in his late teens. If a major trend in American society was the constant and vigorous reappraisal of Old World values, a counter trend was the assertion of those values through the ruling elite of the East Coast. By the 1960s the patent failure of these values to prevent two world wars and to save Europe from domination by a series of repressive dictatorships had exploded the myth of civilisation and the stable society. The young of both the New and the Old Worlds embarked on a search for their own authentic values – one of their major codes of identity was music, particularly rock music.

Back in the 1950s when Bill Haley and the Comets played 'Rock Around the Clock' at the beginning of the film *Blackboard Jungle*, an exuberance of activity was released in the young that was entirely new. The older generation were scandalised by the streams of young people dancing in the cinemas, dancing on the tops of buses and dancing in the streets. Maybe a few rich exhibitionists had danced the Charleston on the top of London taxis, but this time it was a whole generation dancing, revelling and often rumbling. Rock had arrived!

Rock themes are the standard fare of romanticism and the Gothic: pains of love, protests against poverty, coldness of isolation, aberrations of personality, drug-induced hallucinations and so on. The difference lies in the tone, which is raw and untutored. It is no longer assumed that practitioners need to have an extensive formal training in order to make their impact. Neither is it deemed necessary to have a systematic knowledge of the past before you can dare to give utterance yourself. Rock might deal in age-old subjects but its sound is bold, its expression contemporary and the form follows the dictates of the need for immediate impact.

Sam Shepard is by way of being the rock star of American drama and it is my purpose to explore the full implications of this description.

At the most basic level Shepard, like many of his generation, has expressed not only admiration for rock stars but also his desire to be one. In 1975 he toured as observer with Bob Dylan's 'Rolling Thunder Review' and published his experiences in *The Rolling Thunder Logbook*. During the 1960s he played drums with the Holy Modal Rounders, a country-psychedelic group, and his sojourn in London during the early 1970s was expressly for the purpose of getting into rock music. 'I was in a band in New York and I'd heard that this [London] was the rock'n'roll centre of the world – so I came here with that kind of idea.'[1]

Even more important is the significance music has in his plays, not just rock but also jazz, blues, country-and-western and folk. The music is not, as in Brecht, used for alienation but as an integral component in the overall effect. Music underscores the immediacy of the emotional impact: 'it's in the nature of music, it's when you can play a note and there's a response immediately – you don't have to build up to it through seven scenes'.[2] And that is an essential part of Shepard's theatre: he wants it to have the total impact of a rock concert.

Characteristically a rock concert is an immediate visceral experience. The atavistic rhythms of the music, the strutting and posing of the players, the primal scream quality of the voices, the eclectic styles of the costumes and the intensity of the emotions that are their subject matter all conspire to create a moment of experience that has nothing but the vaguest past and no aspirations for a future – it is complete in the present.

Naturally drama has to take account of words which have far more significance than in a rock concert. Words carry with them a history of the culture they both represent and create. But even here Shepard has harnessed the physical reality of words just as much as their meaning component in order to focus the audience's attention. In jazz the soloist plays a riff 'which . . . can control an audience, leading them, with whatever rhythms the player chooses, towards whatever heights or depths the player decides'.[3] Shepard uses the raw physical power of language like the greats of jazz or like a rock star.

Possibly the most succinct account of Shepard's language comes from the poet Patti Smith, with whom he lived for a time:

> the fast moving car
> the engine
> the black mustang pony
> the electric guitar. . . . .
> Out with a new demon . . . rock'n'roll. With an amplifier for
>   a heart he slid into Detroit.
> The motor city: cars and radios.
> His father was a Dixieland drummer
> The roots of his theatre was music too . . .
>
> His theatre encompassed all those rhythm trade-offs all
> those special dialogues of the heart.[4]

In other words, Shepard uses language first and foremost as a poet and a magician. I use the word magician advisedly because his drama is allied to the ceremonious incantations of sympathetic magic that exist at the heart of our earliest cultural manifestations. It is a magic to banish evil and ensure good by enacting the destruction of evil forces and the accomplishment of good. Language becomes an end in itself – language is action.

In the next two sections of this chapter I propose to look at the plays themselves in terms of language and performance. The language is the poetic language of magic rituals and the performance the tribal celebration of a mutual identity.

II

Language consists of the sensuous and the rational: the sensuous is the sound and rhythm of the words, while the rational is the meaning. Although by no means exclusively so, the sensuous is the gateway to poetry while the rational gives rise to the ideas and underlying themes. In Shepard's case, as Richard Gilman points out in his excellent introduction to *Seven Plays*, critics are agreed that there is confusion as to his themes. His substantial body of work does not readily lend itself to a discussion of themes and resolutions. For example, in *Curse of the Starving Class*, Weston, the father, may have pulled himself together by the end of the play but his son Wesley has dressed in his father's old clothes and the debts that Weston has piled up are being reclaimed by gangsters. The final image of the cat and the eagle tearing each other to pieces in mid-air is as sharp, desperate and nihilistic as the darkest moments in, for example, Tennessee Williams.

Shepard is no dramatist as medicine-man touting bottles of elixir to cure human ills. Rather, he is the magician performing rites for human suffering. He has no solution for the pains of the human condition, the monsters lurk always within. But the magician ceremonially joins us in a magic circle of human sympathy and feeling to encourage us in our confrontation with outer darkness. As Shepard himself has said:

> Language is a veil hiding demons and angels which the characters are always out of touch with. Their quest in the play is the same as ours in life – to find those forces, to meet them face to face and end the mystery.[5]

To claim that entering Shepard's theatre is to do no less than enter into the magical rites that constitute the very origins of theatre must, on the surface, appear extravagant or rather grandly metaphorical. My claim is intended to be neither; it is intended to identify the nature of the experience of his theatre and it is intended to be literally true. For the reasons I have already argued, Shepard's theatre is theatre for a new world.

An example of his early work is the 1969 monologue *Voices from the Dead*. Like so many of Shepard's characters, the speaker is an archetypal American figure, the rodeo rider. The event being recalled is the bull riding, the outcome the death of the speaker, who is trampled by the bull. The central situation is the classic confrontation: man trying to tame the dark forces of nature represented from earliest times by the awesome figure of the bull. Moreover, in order to express the primitive nature of the conflict, the rules of the game are off: 'The Rodeo Association made the Suicide Grip illegal in somethin' like 1959 but that didn't stop no bull rider I knew from usin' the damn thing' (p. 183). The rider by strength and cunning (the use of the Suicide Grip) tries to become an inseparable part of the power of the bull: 'You just flap with the bucks like you was an extra piece a skin on that bull's back' (p. 183). But the bull finally breaks the strength of the rider and crushes him into the earth 'sendin' me back where I came from' (p. 184).

Primitive and symbolic though the struggle is, it is not sufficient of itself to constitute what amounts to a religious celebration of the myth of the human condition. The enactment of the myth requires poetic language, the use of the sensuous stuff of language to fully engage the consciousness of the audience. At the sound level there are numerous examples of the fashioning of the phonemes to articulate the events in progress. Take for example: 'When that ch*u*te *o*pens b*o*y y*o*u hang *o*n like ep*o*xy t*o* w*oo*d' (p. 183). In sound terms the underlined phonemes represent virtually all the rounded back vowels in English. Such a collection must be considered to be highly motivated and warranting some explanation. In interpretative terms the sounds express the open-mouthed gasp of the rider suddenly hurled into the space of the arena.

In 'If it's *b*ad he's *g*ot you all *c*rooked and *p*rayin' for *b*alance. A*ch*in' for the *b*ell' (p. 183) the plosive consonants, made by the vocal chords suddenly releasing air in an explosion, express the dramatic and abrupt opening of the conflict between man and bull. But far more important than these effects, which we might call poetic interludes in the monologue, is the sustained poetic structure.

The essential form of the piece is an intricate series of repetitions of which only the most obvious level is the repetition of actual words. Like the psalms, the poetic form derives from the Hebrew form in which key subjects are repeated from different points of view.

(a) Mad as hell
(b) and *he ain't lettin' me go.*
(c) *Not never.*
(d) He's got me this time
(e) and he knows it.
(f) *I ain't never gonna get up again.*
(g) He's makin' me part a the earth.
(h) Mashin' me down.
(i) Pulverizin' my flesh.
(j) Sendin' me back where I come from.   (p. 184)

The three italicised phrases in (b), (c) and (f) represent: (b) the bull won't let the rider go; (c) it is an absolute that the rider won't escape; and (f) the rider acknowledges he won't escape. (a) to (e) represent the situation from the bull's point of view: he has the rider and is aware of it; (f) is a pivotal sentence where the rider admits to the bull's supremacy; and (g) to (j) iterate the rider's submission from different points of view. Line (g) states objectively what is happening to the rider from a world perspective; (h) emphasises the violent and physical connotations; (i) expresses the implications for the rider from a more detached intellectual viewpoint; and (j) gives the implications for the rider at a metaphysical level. All the statements repeat what the rider perceives as happening to him, but each one entails a different perspective. We can argue as to what precisely that perspective is, but finally we see that Shepard is not merely saying the same thing several times, but that each time a different world view is entailed, gradually building a universe out of the fate of the rodeo rider. It is that universe of human fate that connects us to the protagonist and our recognition of it that unites us with audience, author and actor.

In *The Tooth of Crime* Shepard takes the mythic story of the ageing hero and leader being challenged by a young rebel, and places it in a science fiction world – a world suffused by the post-war youth culture of pop and rock music, fast cars and the glamour and glitz of advertising. The mythic core of action is supported by other features which further the sense that the play is also a magic ritual.

Magic rituals are characterised by hierarchical organisation. The ageing hero is Hoss, who is not only the leader but also that most twentieth-century shaman, a rock star. We are in the world of media idols and Hoss is surrounded by his accolytes. He has Becky his handmaiden, a private astrologer, to advise him on the propitiousness of the time, a disc-jockey to tell him where he is in the charts, and a doctor to administer the drugs that keep him cool, make him hot or space him out. Not only do the members of the retinue have particular functions, but these functions are exercised in a highly ritualised fashion, decisions being based on signs and charts.

Crow is the challenger: a gypsy who travels solo and operates outside the arcane roles that govern the 'game' as Hoss knows it and plays it. The first act shows us the magic circle of Hoss. The second act is the duel between Hoss and Crow in which Crow usurps the throne. While the piece appears violent and harsh, its cruelty as in ritual tends to be in attitudes and words rather than in the actual action itself. The battle between Hoss and Crow is a verbal duel in which it is the rules of the game that are overthrown by the solo player who recognises no rules, rather than a physical duel necessarily leading to the death of the loser.

So it is not just the situation located deep in the human psyche and the paraphernalia of ritual roles and behaviour which create the sense of magic, it is also the nature of the play of language. The language invoked is the stylised dialects of two contending generations, say Elvis Presley versus Johnny Rotten. The duel is a war of styles, victory going to Crow who is literally a scavanger of all styles.

The ability of the protagonists to adopt the clichés of hip, Western or gangster talk are reminiscent of the 'speaking in tongues' that is so much a part of fundamentalist religion. The poetry of the language that can be analysed in the same way as my previous account of *Voices from the Dead* contributes to the sense of ritual magic. But above all, the music and songs bind players and audience in the ritual incantation of a litany of beliefs. Crow, the challenger, acknowledges nothing but his need to make a kill, and he is prepared to do whatever success demands. One of the first things he does is to practise Hoss's walk until he has it to perfection. Imitation and parody are his essential skills and he has constructed himself for that purpose. His song repeats three times:

> But I believe in my mask – The man I made up is me
> And I believe in my dance – And my destiny. (p. 232)

From Hoss's song 'The Way Things Are' at the opening of the play, music and song are used to reinforce the mood and meaning of the characters within the drama. Their repetitions, like the refrain in hymns, emphasises the central message or statement out of which the verses grow.

Shepard's plays may get their emotional kick from invoking the rites of tribal magic but they are still plays, not merely rituals. The myth at the centre of the action takes on immediacy by being about real human and contemporary concerns. Hoss is prey to doubts, the rules of the game are also limitations: language gives the possibility of expression but it is also the prison-house of meaning. 'Sure I'm good. I might even be great but I ain't no genius. Genius is something outside the game. The game can't contain a true genius'

(p. 207). Crow on the other hand recognises no obligations to the game: he can triumph because he accepts no limitations in his drive to success. As Hoss says: 'Without a code it's just crime. No art involved. No technique, finesse. No sense of mastery. The touch is gone' (p. 216).

After his defeat by Crow, Hoss shoots the referee and tries to persuade Crow to teach him how to succeed the new way. But he recognises that he cannot become simply an image determined solely by the need to triumph in any situation. Having been overthrown, he shoots himself. In a world where image is all, the old-style star takes himself out of the running:

> Now stand back and watch some true style. The mark of a lifetime. A true gesture that won't never cheat on itself 'cause it's the last of its kind. It can't be taught or copied or stolen or sold. It's mine. An original. It's my life and death in one clean shot. (p. 249)

While Shepard sees clearly the artificiality of the old ways of doing and being in a New World, he is not so naive as to suppose that one can operate in society without a code.

In plays and films since the late 1970s, Shepard has explored the nature of being human through often sensational subject matter such as infanticide, poverty, alchoholism, wife-beating and even success in the movie business. Through all his protagonists runs the mythic heritage, the sense of each particular human being struggling both with his or her environment and with an inner fatal flaw. The fundamental nature of the conflict is accentuated by the primitive nature of the environment in which the exploration so often takes place. In *True West* Lee is limited by the clichés that dominate his thinking, but in the desert can exercise his capacity for doing. Austin, his screen-writer brother, wants to prove himself by living in the desert but does not know how. In *Buried Child* the setting is a run-down farm-house on land that has become increasingly infertile since the 1930s; the same poverty-stricken location is the background to *Curse of the Starving Class*, while the film *Paris, Texas* opens with the jealous alchoholic father striding, mindless and desolate, through the desert.

As in Greek tragedy, the essential social unit is the family, and the stories take their dynamic from troubled family histories. Jake, in *A Lie of the Mind*, loves Beth but very nearly beats her to death through the frustrations of jealousy. Later we learn of his alchoholic, errant father and how the father was killed by a lorry in a drunken race with Jake. He was consumed with 'This deep, deep hate that came from somewhere far away. It was pure black hate with no purpose' (p. 93), a hate that was released when he was drunk and that has in its own way infected Jake. 'These things – in my head – lie to me. Everything lies. Tells me a story. Everything in me lies. But you' (p. 128). At the end all Jake can do is to renounce Beth and give her over to the care of his brother Frankie.

In biblical terms the sins of the fathers are endlessly visited on the children. The only path of hope for the future is through some sacrificial act. In *Paris, Texas* the father restores their son to his estranged wife; in *A Lie of the Mind* Jake gives Beth into Frankie's keeping. Without such renunciations the shadow of the past extends into the future.

III

This summary account of Shepard's subject matter is suggestive of a dour if not traumatic evening at the theatre. In fact, the conditions of performance engender an intensity of audience involvement and a consequent exhilaration that can be likened to true religious believers at worship, or rock fans at a rock festival. These two parallels intentionally point to Shepard's roots in the oldest traditions of drama, namely its relation to myth and magic and to Dionysian frenzy. In the previous section I have tried to suggest some of the ways in which the language is organised to concentrate its effectiveness. Music has also been seen as a powerful force for eliciting emotional response.

But a further characteristic of Shepard's work is its ability to focus on the here and now. The experience of his theatre has no past or future, it is overwhelmingly of the present. It is quite normal for characters to have a past which they bring with them into the play: Hamlet has been to university, Willie Loman has been failing as a salesman over a number of years. In Shepard's plays the motivation for characters to be on the stage is as vague as their past is illusory. In *Fool for Love* we do not know why Mary is in a cheap motel on the edge of the Mojave desert, and we know little more of Eddie who has come over 2000 miles out of his way to see if she is all right. What we know is that they are fully and emotionally on the stage in front of us. We learn that they are children of the same father and so their love is incestuous, but they both have different accounts of how they came by that knowledge. Halie in *Buried Child* remembers her dead son Ansel as a champion basketball player, Bradley on the other hand says, 'He never played basketball' (p. 116). Furthermore, being characters on the edge of society, they are unencumbered by the defining characteristics of class or profession. Even the women characters who aspire to a better way of life, aspire to a gentility that is dream rather than substance.

What is unequivocal about the characters in front of us is the force of their emotions. Stripped bare of social pretensions they are vividly emotional beings playing the life struggle that those emotions engender. The emphasis is on their being rather than doing, and that being is immediately before us on the stage.

Where possible the staging itself is designed to incorporate the audience into the experience. In his original production of *Fool for Love* Shepard had loudspeakers placed under the seating in the auditorium – every crash of the door reverberated through the audience. In *A Lie of the Mind* the opening phone call from Jake to Frankie has Frankie behind the audience. In the Royal Court production telephone wires ran above the heads of the audience. In *The Tooth of Crime* the stage is bare except for the black chair that looks 'something like an Egyptian Pharaoh's throne', creating for the audience the sense of being given an audience by royalty.

Of course, in spite of Shepard's detailed descriptions of staging for his plays, any given production is subject to the vision of a particular director working with a company in a particular place at a particular time. What remains constant is the emotional force of the material reaching out to encompass audience and performers in a celebration of the depth and vitality of the struggle to be human in a New World.

NOTES

The Sam Shepard texts quoted in the essay are 'Voices from the Dead', in *Motel Chronicles and Hawk Moon* (London: Faber & Faber, 1985); *The Tooth of Crime, True West, Buried Child* and *Curse of the Starving Class* in *Seven Plays*, introd. by R. Gilman (New York: Bantam Books, 1984); *Fool for Love* (London: Faber & Faber, 1987); *A Lie of the Mind* (London: Methuen, in association with the Royal Court Theatre, 1987).

1. Sam Shepard 'Metaphors, Mad Dogs and Old Time Cowboys', interview with K. Chubb, reprinted in B. Marranca (ed.), *American Dream: The Imagination of Sam Shepard* (New York: Performing Arts Journal Publications, 1981) p. 200.
2. Ibid., p. 202.
3. S. Jaksic, 'The Disintegrating America of Sam Shepard', unpublished MA thesis, University of Leeds, 1990. I am indebted to Svetlana Jaksic for several discussions about Sam Shepard's work and her 1988 production of *Savage Love*.
4. P. Smith, 'Sam Shepard; 9 Random Years (7 + 2)', in *Angel City, Curse of the Starving Class, and Other Plays* (New York: Urizen Books, 1976) p. 244.
5. Quoted in D. L. Kirkpatrick (ed.), *Contemporary Dramatists*, 4th edn (New York: St Martin's Press, 1988) p. 481.

9

Marsha Norman

DARRYLL GRANTLEY

Marsha Norman first came to public attention in this country in 1984 with the production at the Hampstead Theatre Club of her harrowing play *'night Mother*, a work which won the Pulitzer Prize in 1983 as well as a host of other prizes.[1] This play marked her out as one of the most promising playwrights of her generation. Norman had, however, been writing since the mid 1970s and had been the recipient of a number of other awards for her first play, *Getting Out*, premièred in 1977 and co-winner for that year of the Actors Theater of Louisville's Great American Play Contest. Her next play, *Third and Oak* was performed on stage in Louisville in 1978 and produced later that year on American National Public Radio. The first half of this play was subsequently produced in New York for a one-act play festival, under the title *The Laundromat*. In 1980 Norman developed her next play, *The Holdup*, in an actors' workshop which she directed in Louisville. The play had a subsequent production in New York as well but was officially premièred in San Francisco's American Conservatory Theater in 1983. In that year *'night Mother* was produced on Broadway and this has subsequently been made into a film as well. Her last significant play to date, *Traveller in the Dark*, was first staged at the American Repertory Theater in Cambridge, Massachusetts, in 1984 although since then she has written musical works and lesser plays such as *Winter Shakers* in 1987, *Sarah and Abraham* in 1988, and the collaborative *The Secret Garden*.[2] Norman has refused to allow the publication of another play, *Circus Valentine*, because an only performance was 'a total disaster', and her latest work, *Sarah and Abraham* is as yet unpublished. She has also written a novel, *The Fortune Teller*, published in 1987,[3] as well as screenplays for film and television.

The best of Marsha Norman's work centres around women, and certain of her plays have placed her among the ranks of the prominent American feminist playwrights. This is particularly true of her first piece, *Getting Out*, and her best-known work, *'night*

Mother. Taking her work as a whole, however, she is difficult to view unproblematically in these terms, both because of her subject matter and her mode of writing. It can certainly be claimed that she is at her best in plays which focus on women, and in these she shows herself capable of rendering very powerfully the crises of identity which arise from the position of her women imprisoned in a social structure dominated by patriarchal power and values. She also does at times represent positively relationships of community and support between women. However, in other plays her narrative focus simply reinscribes the patriarchal marginalisation of women, and this is not addressed as an issue. Even in what might be regarded as her most 'feminist' work the politicisation of questions of gender identity and power, to the extent that it occurs at all, is far from explicit. Much of the reason for this proceeds from her preferred mode of writing too: apart from her first play, Norman's writing is entirely in a realist mode. Whereas it is an issue of debate how far conventional realism can serve the purposes of feminist theatre,[4] Norman's adherence to narrative conventions governing the representation of gender role and identity in her realist plays, with possibly the partial exception of *'night Mother*, could be argued to result in an implicit restatement of the patriarchal values which some of her writing seems to challenge. Though her evocative use of stage symbolism and her successful departure from realism in her first play suggest considerable gifts in the direction of more experimental theatre, she is particularly accomplished as a traditional realist writer, and it is perhaps her very dramaturgical conventionality which has facilitated recognition of her considerable talent by the critical establishment. A prominent American critic hailed her as 'an authentic, universal playwright – not a woman playwright mind you, not a regional playwright, not an ethnic playwright, but one who speaks to the concerns of all humankind',[5] a comment which not only claims for her a sort of canonical status as a dramatic writer, but revealingly relegates the other categories mentioned to an inferior order. An observation which Norman herself made about the emergence of women dramatists reveals something of her view of her own work and women's writing in general:

Now we [women] can write plays and not have people put them in a little box labelled 'women's theatre'. It's a time of great exploration of secret worlds, of worlds that have been kept very quiet.[6]

Norman's debut play, *Getting Out*, is one of her most accomplished to date and shows a great deal of promise which has only partially been realised in her subsequent work. It is a powerful piece expressing anger and bitterness but containing too the wryness and light irony which characterises much of her writing. The title refers to the release from an eight-year prison term of the central character, Arlene, delinquent since childhood, imprisoned for the murder of a taxi driver in the course of a petrol-station robbery which also involved the attempted kidnap of an attendant. The play opens just after her release with her arrival at a dingy apartment formerly occupied by her prostitute sister in Louisville, Kentucky. She has been transported by a prison guard who had befriended her and who now seeks to 'take care' of her. The play constantly refers backward in time, and incidents from Arlene's past are represented on stage and juxtaposed with events of the present. The narrative as it relates to the present of the play revolves around the various significant figures with whom Arlene exists in a relationship of real or potential dependence, while the 'past' narrative represents her psychic history, from the conditions of her childhood which led to a state of violent, self-destructive anger to her later evolution from or abdication of this anger in favour of a position of cool, ironic, almost passive detachment. Complicating all of this is her longing for her child, taken from her and fostered, and the repeated disregard shown by others for her feelings as a mother, something which is left unresolved at the end of the play.

The major interest of the play is its powerful feminist subtext: the central figure's experience is represented in such a way as to reveal various forms of oppression in cross-gender relationships: the sexual abuse of Arlene by her father; the crude sexual approaches to the juvenile Arlene by a male fellow inmate at a juvenile institution; the sexual ulterior motives of the 'friendly' prison guard, Bennie; and economic exploitation by the pimp, Carl, who tries to induce Arlene to return to prostitution. There are also different forms of coercion by the prison chaplain, who succeeds in breaking Arlene's rebellious spirit by offering a spurious religious alternative, and by the doctor, whose power resides in sedative drugs.

The two non-cross-gender relationships in the play are also relevant to this perspective. Arlene vainly appeals to her mother for love and help, but it becomes clear that this relationship is made impossible by the damage which both women have sustained, the older woman through her impossible position at the centre of a problem family and with no support from an errant husband. The one relationship which does seem to offer hope in the play is that offered by a fellow ex-convict, Ruby, herself a victim of sexual exploitation and the judicial process. Ruby is the one major figure who is able to offer no material help, but to whose refuge of support Arlene tentatively turns at the end of the play. Ruby's experience in the world of the low-paid, and the dilemma of choice facing Arlene, between material well-being in prostitution or self-respect and poverty, contribute additional aspects to the picture. None of the issues implicit in the narrative is given either any explicit analysis or overt political perspective, but the limitations of the characters in terms of their philosophical view or broader political understanding of their situation is perhaps the most telling political statement of all.[7] The inability of Arlene, the mother and Ruby to extend their perceptions beyond their particular experience, and their hard pragmatism with respect to their circumstances, act along with the manifold images of imprisonment in the play to present a view of women who are not only incarcerated within patriarchal social and economic structures, but whose very identity is formed by those structures.

The play also affords perspectives essentially from women's emotional and material experience. Arlene's dilemma is not simply an economic one, though the extent to which it is so has much to do with her position as a women; it also relates to her history of sexual abuse, her view of herself as a human and sexual being, and to the crisis of her rejection both as daughter and as mother.

In terms of her construction of dramatic character and range of focus, this play exhibits a tendency Norman was to go on to develop in her later pieces, a focus on a small range of characters with a particular interest in the psychology of the central figures. In *Getting Out* the actual number of *dramatis personae* is relatively large by comparison with her later plays, but the effective interest remains in the principal figure of Arlene. In a departure from linear narrative unusual for Norman, she represents her central character in two forms, the Arlene of the present and Arlene in various stages of her past, played by another actor and distinguished by the name Arlie, a form of appellation discarded by Arlene in the process of her reshaping of her identity. These incarnations of Arlene are constantly juxtaposed on stage, with no awareness of each other until (ambiguously) at the end, but the parallels in their actions and attitudes set up many of the ironies and perspectives generated in the play and contributed the physical domination of the stage by the psyche of this composite central figure. It is also effective both in dramatising Arlene/Arlie's history of oppression and its continuance in her state of 'freedom' through a variety of ironic relationships, and in representing graphically the the fragmentation and coercion of female identity in a patriarchal economic and social system. In these ways Norman is able to do what she does best in her dramatic work and in her novel: explore the relationship between one individual and a world with which they are in one way or another at odds, or from which they are alienated. Rather paradoxically, her method in this play also enables her to construct her principal character in terms of the process of transformation which Helene Keyssar argues is central to feminist theatre,[8] though here the transformation in Arlie/Arlene is from anger and resistance to an inward acceptance of the harsh economic and social constraints placed on her life.

Of all her plays to date, *Getting Out* is the one in which Norman makes most varied and fluid use of the stage as an acting and signifying space. Unlike her other plays, which tend to have a much more traditional form of staging in keeping with their more straightforwardly linear narratives, this play moves the action back and forth in time, with various parts of the stage representing simultaneously the different contexts for action, in a way which is comparable with Arthur Miller. The direction tells us, 'a catwalk stretches above the apartment [in which the foreground action is located] and a prison cell, stage right, connects to it by stairways. An area downstage and another stage left complete the enclosure of the apartment by playing areas for the past. The apartment must seem imprisoned.' The last direction indicates the iconographic tendency in Norman's staging, which is to be found in all her plays. Images of imprisonment, both visual and verbal, contribute powerfully to the play's exploration of the brutalisation and progressive ensnaring of the focal character as she repeatedly falls prey to and attempts to resist personal and institutional forms of oppression. It is significant that each of the two acts of the play are preceded by announcements made by a disembodied voice in a 'droning tone' issuing orders and instructions to inmates of a correctional institution. This is very effective in setting a scene in which the frequently personalised forms of coercion invariably have an depersonalised anterior referent, such as institutional rules or the office of the (usually male) authority figures (guard, chaplain, warden, doctor), and in which compassion and concern are at best means to effect conformity and at worst simply fronts for ulterior motives of sexual exploitation. The form of staging in the play also affords many opportunities for the juxtaposition of the circumstances of Arlene's life of the narrative present and incidents from her past, which not only provides a dramatically successful representation of her psychological history and its contextual determinants, but raises many ironic perspectives, particularly relating to correspondences between Arlene's life in prison and her life outside.[9]

The success of *Getting Out* as a play is perhaps attributable to the fact that in it Norman is doing what she does best: the dramatisation of a crisis suffered by a central character who is limited and disempowered. Norman presents no real solution here and even the political analysis is more implicit than explicit, but the perspectives generated from a position of passivity and powerlessness are trenchant in their deconstruction of the oppressive processes of sexual and institutional hierarchies of power. The central character ultimately has power only over herself, itself severely curtailed, and her exercise of that, along with the support of someone equally a victim, are the only small glimmers of hope in a play otherwise uncompromisingly bleak.

The two acts of Norman's next play, *Third and Oak*, might be considered two separate pieces, and one has indeed been reconstituted as a one-act play, though there are correspondences between the two halves as well as other linking elements. The first act is set in a launderette in the early hours of the morning and involves mainly the conversation of two women, one middle-aged and the other younger, in which their lives and marriages are revealed. It emerges towards the end of the scene that the elder, Alberta, has become widowed a year earlier and it is only now that she can bring herself to launder her dead husband's clothes. The conversation of the more voluble Deedee is revealing about the frustrations and inadequacies of her marriage and her appallingly difficult situation as the wife of a crude, boorish man with whom she is none the less in love. However, what is extracted from the more reserved, middle-class Alberta is a picture of a relationship which, though on the surface ideal, is replete with misunderstandings and subtle disharmonies. Both women are alarmed when a dapper young black man enters the launderette and addresses them genially; but when it turns out he is a local disc-jockey, a light flirtation develops between him and Deedee. He announces his intention to go to the pool hall next door while his clothes are in the wash. He invites both women to join him; Alberta declines but Deedee agrees to join him later. It is in the uneasy period after his departure that the two women engage in some conflict and through this to some understanding of and sympathy with each other.

The second act, in the pool hall, is equally simple in structure and consists basically of a dialogue between the disc-jockey, Shooter, and the pool hall owner, Willy, who was an old friend of Shooter's father. Three main issues emerge from the exchanges which are at once rancorous and affectionate and largely retrospective. The first is Shooter's identity problems, which arise principally from his own discontentment and his identification with his dead father, an ace pool player. The second is his troubled marriage to the daughter of George who, along with Willy and Shooter's father, formed a triumvirate of close friends known as the 'three blind mice'. The third is the future of the pool hall and the friendship of Willy and George. Shooter thinks Willy is selling the pool hall to retire elsewhere and abandon George, who is ill, but it later emerges that he is selling it to finance a comfortable end to George's life, because it turns out that he has only six months to live. Deedee enters towards the end of the act with Shooter's cleaned and dried clothes, which she has folded. The flirtation continues and they almost go out together for a late snack, but Willy's clear objection to this forces Shooter to abandon the plan and Deedee goes home to her husband, who has at last returned.

In some ways the play might be seen as attempting to engage too many issues and knitting together two episodes which are not sufficiently connected, thus compromising its unity and focus. It might even be regarded as the uneasy marriage of essentially a pair of two-handers, with the the rather clumsy device of a character more centrally placed in the other half coming in as a sort of intruder to link the two sections. However, there is an obvious parallel as the older protagonist in each half acts as a confessor to the younger (though neither exchange is that one-sided). The play also deals with the difficulties of institutionalised cross-gender relationships: the marriages of Deedee, Shooter and even Alberta, and contrasts these implicitly with the powerful commitment in the looser friendship of Willy and George, the strong bond between Willy and Shooter or even the quick understanding and sympathy arrived at in the casual encounter of Alberta and Deedee. This does produce a perspective on the institution of marriage which has some feminist implications but of the remotest possible kind. Whereas in the case of Deedee the imprisonment of a powerless woman in the loneliness of a loveless marriage and her reduction to the status of a child is clearly presented, there is little real attempt to represent or suggest the institutional causes of this; the problem remains on the level of personality. The situation is further complicated by the contrast with Alberta, the loss of whose husband has left her bereft and lonely, and not enough information is provided to respond to this except on the level of sentiment.

Though there are hints of *malentendu* in this relationship too, they are drawn into the poignancy of the loss rather than providing any convincing point of departure for any more profound view. The narrative defines both women in relation to men, and more specifically the absence of the men who validate their lives. Deedee's relationship also contrasts with Shooter's marriage to a beautiful but grasping yuppie. Here again there is some attempt at a perspective in Willy's view of the marriage, but we are left with little to go on apart from the opinions of a character as limited in vision as any other, and so no very trenchant analysis is forthcoming. Both Deedee and Shooter express the desire for children, with the clear implication that it would be a way of addressing their loneliness and lack of a sense of identity, but they are frustrated in this by their partners' refusal in the face of conflicting personal interests outside of marriage.

While it is difficult to pursue very far the issues raised in this play, Norman is very skilled at delineating not only her stage characters but also their situations through deft and evocative dramatic touches. The class difference between Alberta and Deedee, for instance, is evinced by a number of telling details, such as Deedee's refusal of a proffered magazine saying she has brought instead a Dr Pepper (a fizzy drink) and the misfiring of a joke by Alberta which depended on knowing who Herbert Hoover was. The dramatic qualities of the play are enhanced by the tensions aroused by the various misunderstandings and contrasts in values of the two women, and these throw into greater relief the understanding and sympathy of each for the other's predicament; here the community of women transcends the divisions of class.

Another instance of a small dramatic detail which reveals a great deal is Shooter's entry into the launderette and the effect this has on the two women, elaborated in the discussion they have about it after his departure. Such details locate the immediate interest in the dramatic presence of the characters on stage but this presence also allows Norman a level of understatement in terms of the ideas which amounts to the eschewing of implications naturally generated by the situations she represents. Thus there is a denouement to each act which affirmatively closes off a situation that has little or nothing inherently optimistic about it. In these instances the sort of passive detachment which runs through Norman's work is unequal to addressing effectively the issues of the genesis or possible resolution of the problems in which her characters are enmeshed.

In keeping with the play's straightforward realist mode and simple linear plot, the use of the stage is very conventional. There are simply two naturalistic sets: the run-down, inner-city launderette and the seedy, decayed pool hall, both empty in the early hours. However, Norman's sets are always at the very least evocative and verge on the symbolic, and these in particular might easily be conceived of in terms of Edward Hopper's bleak urban landscapes. The requirements for both sets are laid out in detail, with the stress on the tawdriness. As in *'night Mother*, Norman is very specific about the time: a clock in the launderette shows 3 a.m. and continues to run through the performance. The locations themselves are by their nature important signifiers: as images of urban transience and loneliness, and decline and loss respectively, the sets for the two acts are very effective contexts for the action played out in them. The launderette is not only an appropriate meeting ground for the three highly diverse characters but has built into it the both the tensions and possibilities for intimacy which are exploited in the play. The faded pool hall also works well both in terms of the specific history and aspirations of Shooter, and in the evocation of a powerful sense of decline and isolation by implicit comparison with its more vivacious past.

In this play and elsewhere Norman exhibits something of Tennessee Williams's sense of the lyricism of setting. Like Williams, she is capable of excess: the first act opens with the final record being played on a radio station about to close, 'Stand by Your Man', and the second with 'The Star-Spangled Banner' being played on a television set in the pool hall at the close of broadcasting.

In 1980 Marsha Norman directed a workshop at the Actors' Theater of Louisville and in that workshop developed her next play, *The Holdup*. This work is somewhat unusual among Norman's published plays to date in that it is set in a period not contemporary with that in which the play is written. The period is, in fact,

1914 and the play looks back to the last days of the Wild West and
forward to the impending First World War. The narrative revolves
around four people. Henry, a cowhand who is stuck in a rut, and
is unmarried at 30, works with a wheat-threshing crew to supple-
ment his income and escapes from the barrenness in his life by
reading outlaw books. Working with him is his teenage brother,
Archie, a naive, garrulous and sweet-natured boy. They are alone
together in the threshing crew's remote cookhouse when they are
held up by an ageing outlaw, a member of a dying breed, who
demands food. He was come to meet an old flame at this prear-
ranged spot and she duly arrives soon after: Lily, a former belle and
now hotel owner in the nearby town. The rambling and rather
whimsical narrative includes the killing of Henry by the Outlaw
in a draw, his burial, the attempted suicide of the Outlaw and
his rescue by Archie and Lily, Lily's seduction of Archie and the
departure of the three survivors, the Outlaw and Lily together,
and Archie off to the war.

Although the play is in certain formal ways in the mould of
Norman's other work – the concentrated focus on a small range of
characters, the division into two acts, and a wry humour which
pervades the writing – it also bears the hallmarks of a piece evolved
in a workshop. Ironically, this works to its detriment rather than
providing it with the input of experience from which many feminist theatre pieces developed in similar circumstances haved ben-
efited. Though the characters are all fully delineated, all striving for
a form of self-realisation within the parameters of their own limitations in terms either of perception or capacities (squarely Norman
territory) there is less evocation of that psychic tension which characterises many of her figures. Instead, the characters appear to have
evolved around more actorly concerns.

Certainly there is a great deal more stage business in this play
than in her others, and there is a strong tendency for the characters
to evolve according to certain defined qualities on which actors
playing them might exercise themselves. Hence Archie is exag-
geratedly an *ingenu*, the Outlaw is almost a caricature Will West
figure, and Lily is cast in very stereotypical terms of mother/lover,
a representation which goes curiously unchallenged in a piece which
otherwise does contain some ironic perspectives on male machismo.
Rather significantly, perhaps, the subject matter of the play came to
Norman through a form of patriarchal transmission, having been
based on stories of outlaws told to her by her grandfather. One

character with potential interest is the frustrated and insecure Henry, but insufficient space is allowed to develop this figure and he is disposed of before the end of the first act. A problem is perhaps the use of figures drawn from American cultural mythology, so that it is difficult to go beyond familiar representations to explore psychological conflicts and tensions.

One idea which Norman does develop with some success in the play, and which is consistent with an 'actorly' piece conscious of its own processes of representation, is that of the construction of self through narrative. The central figure in this is, of course, Henry, who lives imaginatively through outlaw narratives; he becomes increasingly fascinated by the Outlaw until he is drawn into his own narrative and becomes so distanced from reality that he provokes a duel in which he is killed. Storytelling is very important in the play, and before the duel Henry responds to the Outlaw's request for him to tell a story about himself, later trying to force the Outlaw to tell him a story in return.[10] The holdup itself, halfway through Act I, and the parodic funeral of Henry are instances when reality is enacted according to the formula of narrative. Stories are told throughout, including one which Lily tells Archie and this is followed by an interesting and telling piece of dialogue:

ARCHIE: Why didn't you tell me this before?

LILY: It's the only story I know. I was saving it for you.

ARCHIE: It's the best story I ever heard.

LILY: There are plenty more out there. All you have to do is get on the train.

ARCHIE: Things happen here. Things are changing here too. I want to be here when it happens. People like me have to stay here and make it happen.

LILY: When it happens here, Archie, it will be secondhand. But I'm not going to say any more about it. You know what I think. Now, tell me how your brother got his hand eaten by the catfish?[11]

Here experience is conceived of in terms of narrative, but this is closely related to the constitution of identity in these terms as well. This becomes explicit not only in the example of Henry, but with the Outlaw as well. He has an old satchel with him, the contents of which are referred to but not revealed to the audience until near the end, when Archie discovers that it contains 'wanted' posters and newspaper articles about the Outlaw. Archie throws these things on the fire, announcing formally, 'All the outlaws are dead. McCarty [the Outlaw] was an outlaw. McCarty must be dead.' The Outlaw's awareness of his life as narrative, and particularly its place within an emerging American cultural mythology, is an important aspect of the play's negotiation of the complex and blurred line between experienced reality and representation.

This is interesting for its metatheatrical implications, but it is perhaps of most significance when viewed in the context of American culture in the 1980s. Norman wrote this play at the beginning of a decade which saw the Reagan phenomenon, a decade in which a B-movie actor achieve one of the most sustainedly popular presidencies in US history by making America 'feel good about itself' in the face of all economic and social reality. Norman is not the first US playwright or writer to examine the American cultural aspiration to reconstitute social and individual reality in terms of (usually idealised) representations of that reality: the issue of the 'American Dream' crops up regularly in the work of dramatists from O'Neill to Mamet. What Norman fails to do is give it a social or political dimension, and even in so far as it is dealt with from the point of view of personal identity, the exploration does not go far in psychological or existential terms: this is a case of understatement without the further implicit meaning which might be expected to be generated by it.

Despite these limitations, there are aspects of Norman's writing and dramaturgy which go a long way towards making the play theatrically interesting. There is a great deal of gentle comedy throughout, much of it being produced by incongruities in the response of characters to situations, such as Archie's 'What am I going to tell mother' when his brother is killed, or the Outlaw's response to Archie's recitation of 'The Lord is My Shepherd' at Henry's funeral, 'Are we through now? I ain't prayin' to no sheepherder.' The set is simple, an isolated cookshack in a flat New Mexico landscape in a scene that 'looks almost pre-Civil War'. This provides an atmospherically appropriate backdrop for a drama of lonely, directionless, limited people searching for a destiny beyond their mediocre or exhausted lives. Like Sam Shepard, Norman draws on images from the mythology of the American West, images which she handles ironically while also exploiting the associations which naturally attach to them.

Marsha Norman's acknowledged masterpiece to date is the

Pulitzer prize-winning *'night Mother*, a remarkable piece by any standards. The plot is very simple and the action continues from beginning to end without a break. It concerns a mother and her early-middle-aged daughter who live together in an isolated house on a country road. The daughter, Jessie, is seen making preparations for something, and soon after the opening of the play she reveals to her mother the fact that she is preparing to commit suicide later that evening. What follows is the rest of the evening during which the mother's reactions change from disbelief to supplication and finally to a sort of numbed acceptance. Constantly Jessie busies herself making provision for her mother's comfort after her death, and in the painful and searching discussion which follows the revelation, not only are the reasons for the impending suicide divulged but the two women comb over the bleak emotional history of the family and the even bleaker recent circumstances of Jessie's life: her epilepsy and general bad health, her failed marriage and wayward, criminal son, and the unsatisfactory relationship between Jessie and her brother, Dawson, and sister-in-law, Loretta. What emerges pre-eminently, however, is the mental oppression suffered by Jessie in her relationship with her mother, herself damaged by a loveless marriage and now emotionally dependent on her daughter. This is a relationship of symbiotic entrapment.

Norman's evocative writing is at its best in this play in which she constructs a picture of family failure compounding itself, the family as an emotional minefield. This is represented in various ways, the most immediate being the onstage relationship between Jessie and her mother. The curious reversal of parent–child dependence; it becomes clear from the mother's passion for sweets, her 'treats' which are visibly present all the way through, and the petulant self-centredness which shows clearly through her concern for Jessie, that her own emotional maturation has been stunted. At one point the mother begs Jessie to postpone her suicide just until she herself has died; it is constantly apparent that her fear of Jessie's death is entirely a selfish one. Jessie's care of her mother is represented by the detailed arrangements which she makes for the continued running of the household after her death, and the comprehensiveness of these is an indicator of the degree of responsibility which she has as well as suggesting the extent of her premeditation. Significantly, arrangements for a continued supply of her mother's treats figure prominently in these. On stage Jessie is constantly engaged in chores, while her mother is passive; another image is the regular manicure which Jessie gives her mother, and which they prepare for though it never actually takes place, images of care and nurture which reverse the expected mother–daughter relationship. The only instance of an image of this care being reciprocated is when the mother makes hot chocolate for Jessie and herself, a comfort which fails because neither ends up drinking it. However, the mutuality of the dependence is indicated by the mother's admission that she has let Jessie take charge to give her a purpose in life; and other admissions are made which reveal the mother's protectiveness towards her. The relationship is certainly very fundamental and it has been argued that the play self-consciously addresses a female audience in focusing on issues of female identity and autonomy, particularly on the processes which women need both to identify with and detach themselves from their mothers in order to acquire a 'normal' gendered identity.[12]

Other ways in which the barrenness of the family's emotional life is revealed are through the facts that are brought to light about Jessie's relationship with her brother and his wife, and the discussion which arises about the family's life during Jessie's childhood. Most revealing about the brother, Dawson, is the fact that he always gives Jessie the same present for her birthday, slippers which are too small for her. She engineers that it should be revealed to him after her death that she has never worn them. This instance is part of a catalogue of petty insensitivities and resentments which are built into the play's representation of family life, and though not especially notable in themselves, when placed in the context of family failure they add significantly to the dismal picture which emerges. Far more important is the candid discussion between Jessie and her mother of the life of the family during Jessie's childhood and subsequently, an analysis convincingly provoked by the crisis in which the two women find themselves. The discussion is fired both by the desperate search by the mother for reasons for her daughter's discussion, and Jessie's interest in exploiting her mother's new willingness to talk candidly. The discussion discloses to the audience the material facts of Jessie's own broken marriage and delinquent son, and the epilepsy of both Jessie and her father, but what it brings to the surface about those things which have not come to actual material crisis is far more telling. These things include the quiet estrangement between Jessie's parents, the chronic lack of communication and distance between members of the family, covert rivalry and jealousy, resentment and misunderstanding. What results is a picture of a family of mediocre, limited people unable to understand one another but capable of enormous, unconscious harm. The sense of mediocrity is reinforced throughout, particularly in the characterisation of the mother whose mind rarely rises above trivia. When she accuses Jessie of bringing her misery on herself, Jessie replies that she is intending to do something about it, to which the mother's reply is very characteristic:

> MAMA: Not something like killing yourself. Something like . . . buying us all new dishes! I'd like that. Or maybe the doctor would let you get a driver's licence now, or I know what let's do right this minute, let's rearrange the furniture.[13]

The trivial level of much of the conversation operates dramatically on several levels. It sometimes works comically and the juxtaposition of the very ordinary with the extraordinary event being proposed is extremely effective in throwing the whole episode into a chilling relief, but it also betrays a sort of hopeless irremediability about the situation because of the limitation of the protagonists. This is tragedy of the ordinary at its best.

Even though Norman very skilfully creates this context for her central figure, the principal dramatic force and main ideas in the play reside in the character of Jessie, who is in a situation of quiet and controlled despair. She is, like several of Norman's other characters, powerless even over the circumstances of her own life. She also has a quality of perceptive passivity which is also found in the central figure of Norman's only novel to date, *The Fortune Teller*, and to a greater or lesser extent informs several of her other characters. Here the circumstances of Jessie Cates's life and death naturally contain many implications relating to her experience and disempowerment as a woman, as in *Getting Out*, but her predicament is not represented from a feminist perspective. Instead the playwright places the focus on the question of the control of an individual over her destiny in a way which is much more affirmative of the American individualist ethic than anything else. A striking metaphor at the centre of the play emphasises this:

> JESSIE: Mama, I know you used to ride the bus. Riding the bus and it's hot and bumpy and crowded and too noisy and more than anything in the world you want to get off and the only reason in the world you don't get off is it's still fifty blocks

from where you're going? Well, I can get off right now if I want to, because even if I ride fifty more years and get off then, it's them same place when I step down to it. Whenever I feel like it, I can get off. As soon as I've had enough, it's my stop. I've had enough.[14]

Later in the play another point is made which also emphasises this idea of suicide as a lifestyle option:

MAMA: Look, maybe I can't think of what you should do, but that doesn't mean there isn't something that would help. *You* find it. *You* think of it. You can keep trying. You can get brave and try some more. You don't have to give up!

JESSIE: I'm *not* giving up! This *is* the other thing I'm trying. And I'm sure there are some other things that might work, but *might* work isn't good enough anymore. I need something that *will* work. *This* will work. That's why I picked it.[15]

Jessie's suicide is thus implicitly presented as a positive choice freely and rationally arrived at, and also as the right of an individual to make a fundamental decision about her life. The central ideas in this play are perhaps especially relevant to the current debates around voluntary euthanasia in the US and elsewhere, though Norman does not seek to engage that issue. The effect, however, of placing the dramatic emphasis on the rationality and consideredness of the protagonist's actions is to divert the attention somewhat from the fact of the intolerable circumstances which give rise to it, even though the facts of Jessie's life are revealed. Although these are shown as ultimate determinants, her action is taken when she is relatively disengaged from them ('Waited until I felt good enough') and the logic of her argument emphasises the element of choice. This cool detachment is rather typical of Norman's dramatic characters, something which, though it contributes to the dramatic force of her work and gives an especially chilling quality to this play, tends to close off rather than generate implications. Norman's own comments are again significant here: 'I'm not interested in writing about indulgence of any kind and I'm not interested in anyone who feels he is a victim.'[16] This betrays a sort of square-jawed American individualism which is hardly likely to open up room for a more complex view of social relations.

Technically, Norman's dramaturgy is at its finest in this play; the simplicity of the staging and spareness of the writing contribute a great deal to the considerable power of the piece. Much is conveyed to the audience by the set which depicts a 'relatively new house built way out on a country road'. Norman's directions are very specific:

> The living room is cluttered with magazines and needlework catalogues, ashtrays and candy dishes. Examples of Mama's needlework are everywhere – pillows, afghans, and quilts, doilies and rugs, and they are quite nice examples. The house is more comfortable than messy, but there is quite a lot to keep in place here. It is more personal than charming. It is not quaint. Under no circumstances should the set and its dressing make a judgement about the intelligence and taste of Jessie and Mama. It should simply indicate that they are very specific real people who happen to live in a particular part of the country.[17]

The clutter here is, in its way, a very important signifier and the 'comfort' so assiduously sought by the mother becomes an increasingly ironic visual context to the action of the play.[18] The whole emphasis here is on ordinariness and blandness, and Norman goes on to direct that 'Heavy accents, which would further distance the audience from Jessie and Mama, are also wrong', thus further removing any distancing individuality and specificity from her characters. She was also insistent that the two roles should not be taken by stars for the first Broadway production because 'the audience would see the stars rather than the characters'.[19]

'night Mother is a play which has had a phenomenal success. It has been produced in several countries, translated into 23 languages, made into a feature film and has won for Norman the first Pulitzer Prize for a woman dramatist in 25 years. In foregrounding problems of female identity and the mother–daughter relationship it is a powerful dramatisation of women's experience and the very fact of the enormous success of the play is perhaps its greatest contribution to the feminist theatrical repertoire, since it helps to place female subjectivity firmly on the international dramatic agenda. There remains clearly the problem that the play fails to challenge or subvert the dominant patriarchal ideology which constrains and determines the lives of the women represented, and it eschews any real political analysis of their situations. However, it has been argued that, to the extent that women might conceive their experience of the play in political terms, a feminist theory of reception might re-evaluate it as a feminist text.[20]

Norman's most recent published play to date is *Traveller in the Dark*, first staged in 1984 at the American Repertory Theatre in Cambridge, Massachusetts. It too is a play concerned with loss of faith, but in very different terms. The play has four characters: Sam, a famous surgeon, Glory his wife, Stephen his twelve-year-old son, and Everett his country-preacher father. A further character, Mavis, a childhood friend of Sam's and later a hospital nurse working with him, is also obliquely present through the part she plays in the narrative. It is her funeral which constitutes the main 'event' of the play, though this takes place offstage. As in Norman's other dramatic works, however, the focus also extends very broadly over events anterior to those in the present of the play. The immediate narrative involves Sam's arrival at a decision to divorce Glory, and is concerned also with his relationships with his son and his father. By the end, Sam and Glory have reached an understanding and reconciliation.

There is a considerable problem of focus in this piece since it attempts to deal with a great many issues at once. The immediate business of the play revolves around Sam, and specifically his failing marriage and his relationships with both his father and his son, in terms of his loss of faith. There is also the question of the relationship of all four characters with the dead Mavis, and it is difficult to discern the centre of interest in the play. Sam's difficulty with his marriage arises from a number of factors, including his idealisation in very stereotypical terms of his own mother who died when he was still a child, and his childhood and professional relationship with the saintly Mavis. Images of sacrificial women abound in the play; in addition to the self-denying Mavis and Sam's rosy-cheeked, cookie-baking mother, Glory is described as:

> a lovely woman, who takes her responsibilities as a wife and mother quite seriously. She speaks quickly and laughs easily. She is blessed with rare grace, and elegance of spirit, and nobody understands how on earth she has stayed married to Sam for all these years.[21]

Her understanding and appreciation of Mavis's love and support for Sam contribute to a picture which the play presents of three women who revolve around an essentially egocentric, if gifted man, all in conventional, institutionally determined positions. Any feminist reading of the play would expose this essentially phallocentric and phallogocentric construction of the narrative, particularly since there is insufficient focus on the inner lives and experiences of the women concerned for the representation effectively to problematise the confined and marginalised roles of these women within the narrative.

The play is largely concerned with Sam's relationship with his own father and his son. The question of religion is used to illustrate this, as well as being in itself, if rather lamely, indicative of Sam's lack of any spiritual direction as a 'traveller in the dark'. His resistance to his father is represented in terms of his rebellion against religious belief, and his rigorously rationalist instruction of his own son (as, for instance, in his rather deconstructive approach to nursery rhymes and fairy stories) is used to suggest his attempt to mould the boy in his own terms. There are many ironic parallels in the two father–son relationships, exposing not only the destructiveness of parental possessiveness but the lack of introspective awareness which gives rise to it. The order of the writing here is not, however, of anything like the order of *'night Mother* where similar issues are dealt with, partly because the relatively more complex situation constructed does not allow for the relentless intensity of that play. It is also partly because Norman is at her best in exploring the frustrations and predicaments of her women characters, whose powerlessness produces a revealing inwardness and whose contradictory positions within a patriarchal social structure constitute a natural dynamic for trenchant dramatic representation. The identity problems of her men tend to centre around specific issues such as an competitiveness in terms of prowess, power or ideas between fathers and sons (in this play and *Third and Oak*) or other more explicit forms of competition between men (in *The Holdup*). Though there is some implicit political comment here, Norman tends to negotiate the experience of men in terms which are determined by patriarchal definitions of gendered identity, rather than disclosing their contradictions.

In all the plays which centre on a male subject, Norman's women become theatrically marginalised and reduced in a way which parallels their sociopolitical status (Deedee in *Third and Oak* who enters carrying Shooter's folded clothes; Lily, significantly the only character without a surname in *The Holdup*; Glory in *Traveller in the Dark* constructed in terms of physical beauty and passive motherly grace). In this way the form she uses and the way she chooses to use it can be seen classically to reinscribe patriarchal ideology. The narrative also has, in *Traveller in the Dark*, the effect of consigning to silence and invisibility a character with far more potential dramatic power, particularly from Marsha Norman's pen, than her central character. This is the dead Mavis, who is sketched in through her relationship with all four live characters, and whose identity is only defined in terms of her marginality. Indeed, the play compels an appreciation of Mavis for such qualities as self-denial and life-long dedication with little real reward, a preparedness to serve quietly at the sidelines, qualities which not only produce an approval for accommodation to exploitation and powerlessness, but which also allow her to join another absent character in the play, Sam's dead mother, as a stereotype of gendered identity.

If in terms of purely technical dramaturgy, *Traveller in the Dark* exhibits in some ways aspects of her competence as a dramatist, it is in several other respects a less successful play than most of Norman's other work. She does again make effective use of the single set, a dilapidated garden developed by Sam's mother but neglected since her death. This is exploited in several ways, not only as symbolic of the central figure's childhood past, but his disordered present life; at one point Sam tidies the garden in which remnants of his youth still lie, and at another he starts cutting the weeds. There is never any symbolic overstatement, but the garden remains an evocative context for the drama which is played out in it. There are also the manifold cultural associations of the *hortus conclusus*, particularly to do with lost innocence, and the religious implications are significant in a play which deals with lost faith.

What is perhaps less successful is the degree of contrivance in the ordering of the narrative, such as the somewhat too pointed juxtaposition between Sam's resistance of his father and his attempt to possess the mind and exclusive love of his own son. Certain revelations come too quickly and clumsily, such as Sam's announcement that he intends to divorce Glory or the various revelations surrounding a loan made to Glory by Mavis. Less than accomplished, too, is the character of the boy Stephen, whose naïveté in his questions about the fairy tales is improbable in a bright twelve-year-old, even one who has been denied acquaintance with such stories. Whatever the merits or otherwise of realism, Norman is usually very competent at realist narrative, but in these instances she allows her writing to become clumsy in the interests of driving home certain points. A combination of straight realism with more experimental forms of representation might have suited her purposes better here, as in *Getting Out*.

Another problem is the ending of the play. In a work in which so many highly problematic issues are either raised or reside implicitly in the text, an ending which contrives to be so neatly affirmative is far too 'pat' and even mawkish. The reconciliations all round in the final scene are hard to swallow and the religious tone of the last few lines takes this affirmation into the realms of the ridiculous. Serious American drama more often than not challenges the simplistic forms of affirmative closure found in the more commercial forms of dramatic product, but this play falls squarely into the trap of anodyne denouement.

Marsha Norman's work ranges over a variety of settings and situations but her fundamental interest remains in all her plays the psychology of the individual in some way at odds with her or his world: a young delinquent struggling to make her way in an institutionally hostile and oppressive world in *Getting Out*, a woman isolated by the death of her husband, another struggling with the oppression of a harsh and loveless marriage, and a man with a crisis of identity and an unhappy marriage in *Third and Oak*, a man who, unreconciled to his work and identity as a wheat thresher, lives in the world of outlaw books, and an outlaw who has lived beyond his time in *The Holdup*, a woman whose lack of accommodation to the world leads her to commit suicide in *'night Mother* and a man whose loss of faith is not just religious in *Traveller in the Dark*. Even in her novel *The Fortune Teller* the central character is a seer whose clairvoyance places her in a problematic relationship with the world around her, she is a character with the same comprehending passivity as Jessie in *'night Mother*. This disjunction between individual consciousness and identity and the contexts of values, social practice, economic structures and beliefs in which it is placed has great potential for a profound exposure of the ideological processes determining and constraining individual identity. She said of the emergence of women dramatists in the 1970s and 1980s:

> Plays require active central characters. Until women saw themselves as active, they could not write for the theatre. We are the central characters in our lives. That awareness had to come before women can write about it.[22]

However, Norman's drama largely evades any subversion of the hierarchies of power and values which so oppress her characters; this remains essentially drama of personal crisis, and whatever broader social ideas emerge do so only by the most indirect of implication in most of her plays. This results as much from her particular style as from the realist mode in which she writes; her style has a wryness and calm assurance which bespeaks her tight authorial control over her material, a control which works to close off rather than open up meaning in her texts. While she may be very adept at representing the 'secret worlds that have been kept very quiet', those worlds remain largely severed from the larger sociopolitical contexts which determine their existence.

NOTES

1. Marsha Norman, *'night Mother* (British edition, London: Faber & Faber, 1984).
2. Marsha Norman, *Getting Out, Third and Oak, The Holdup* and *Traveller in the Dark,* in *Four Plays* (New York: Theater Communications Group, 1988).
3. Marsha Norman, *The Fortune Teller* (New York: Random House, 1987).
4. See Helene Keyssar, *Feminist Theatre* (London: Macmillan, 1984) pp. xi–xvi, 1–21.
5. Robert Brustein, review of *'night Mother*, in *New Republic*, issue 3553, (2 May 1983) pp. 25–7.
6. Marsha Norman, Interview with Mel Gussow, 'New Voices in the Theatre', *New York Times Magazine*, 1 May 1983, pp. 22–39, esp. p. 39.
7. Richard Scharine argues for this play as political theatre, which he defines as theatre which 'shows public policy, laws, or unquestioned social codes impinging unfairly and destructively upon private lives', and he makes extensive reference to the position of women in the US prison system ('Caste Iron Bars: Marsha Norman's *Getting Out* as Political Theatre', in J. Redmond (ed.), *Themes in Drama 11: Woman in Theatre* (Cambridge: Cambridge University Press, 1989) pp. 185–98. See also Timothy Murray, 'Patriarchal Panopticism or the Seduction of a Bad Joke: *Getting Out* in Theory', *Theatre Journal*, vol. 35 (1983) pp. 376–88; and Madonna Miner, ' "What's These Bars Doin' Here?" – The Impossibility of *Getting Out*', *Theatre Annual*, vol. 40 (1985) pp. 115–37.
8. Helene Keyssar argues that 'Drama that embraces transformation inspires and asserts the possibility for change; roles and role-playing, not hidden essences, merits attention; we are what we do and what we become, and no-one, neither woman nor man, is restricted from becoming other' (*Feminist Theatre*, p. xiv).

9. Patricia Schroeder points out that in the use of the inner proscenium parallel to the exterior arch of the stage, Norman has 'visualized in a theatrical context Arlene's continuing imprisonment in a limited and limiting social order', and goes on to discuss the metaphor of the theatre as a prison, in 'Locked Behind the Proscenium: Feminist Strategies in *Getting Out* and *My Sister in This House*', *Modern Drama*, vol. 32, no. 1 (March 1989) pp. 104–14.

10. Storytelling is, in fact, a significant element in all Norman's plays. Lisa McDonnell identifies this interest in narratives as characteristic of writers rooted in the southern oral tradition ('Diverse Similitude: Beth Henley and Marsha Norman', *Southern Quarterly*, vol. xxv, no. 3 (Spring 1987) pp. 95–104).

11. Norman, *Holdup*, pp. 150–1.

12. Jenny Spencer, 'Norman's *'night Mother*: Psycho-drama of Female Identity', *Modern Drama*, vol. 30, no. 3 (September 1987) pp. 364–75. See also Spencer, 'Marsha Norman's She-Tragedies', in L. Hart (ed.), *Making a Spectacle: Feminist Essays in Contemporary Women's Theatre* (Ann Arbor, Mich.: University of Michigan Press, 1989) pp. 147–65.

13. Norman, *'night Mother*, p. 34.

14. Ibid., p. 33.

15. Ibid., p. 75.

16. Norman, interview with Gussow, p. 39.

17. Norman, *'night Mother*, p. 4.

18. Frank Rich in his review of the Broadway production, reported that the set by Heidi Landesman was 'right out of a television sitcom' but when the 'cruelly bright lighting' (by Sam Ingalls) came up the house appeared 'colourless and dead' (*New York Times*, 1 April 1983, p. C.3).

19. Norman, interview with Gussow, p. 37.

20. This argument was made by Jeanie Forte in 'Realism, Narrative and the Feminist Playwright: a Problem of Reception', *Modern Drama*, vol. 32, no. 1 (March 1989) pp. 115–25. Jenny Spencer (see note 12) makes a related point, and both discuss the different reception of the play by many men. There have been favourable evaluations by male reviewers, but see Stanley Kauffman, 'More Trick than Tragedy', *Saturday Review* (Sept. 1983) pp. 47–8; Clive Barnes, ' *'night Mother* is a Long Day's Night', *New York Post*, April 1983, p. 37; Robert Asahina, 'The Real Stuff', *Hudson Review*, vol. 37 (Spring 1984) pp. 100–1; and the review by Richard Gilman in *Nation*, 7 May 1983, p. 586.

21. Norman, *Traveller in the Dark*, p. 161.

22. Norman, interview with Gussow, p. 26.

10

David Mamet

EDWARD J. ESCHE

This chapter attempts to move away from a critical perspective that necessitates making absolute decisions about an entire play and towards an approach that is more open to the moment of audience response in the theatre. It follows Jocelyn Trigg's suggestions for further research on David Mamet by describing the playwright's own dramatic theory, and then discussing the technique of audience participation in Shakespeare's problem plays as a possible influence on Mamet's ideas.[1] The chapter concludes by applying the theoretical approach developed to two particular moments in *American Buffalo* and *Reunion*.

I

A considerable amount of criticism on drama addresses its material as if it were a static piece of writing. No doubt, for written texts or scripts of plays this is a perfectly legitimate methodology, time-honoured with such phrases as 'words on the page', but when speaking of a 'play', the fact of the live performance continually moving through time is often considered only slightly or even ignored. Thus, we often find plays read as bearing 'messages', or they have a 'final effect': *American Buffalo* shows the 'possibilities for communion between men destroyed by "business" pressures' and 'we are left in . . . *American Buffalo* . . . with a pessimistic sense of the possibilities of human relationships'.[2] Perhaps so, but this kind of criticism, which is by far in the majority of writing on Mamet, does not address itself to what happens to an audience through the lineal time event of spectating. It also places a heavy emphasis upon the didactic element in the 'final response', and does not consider the sometimes ambiguous element of immediate response to moments in the plays.

The experience of a performed play is not static, even when we know the entire script or 'what happens at the end'. Take, for example, a production of *Measure for Measure*, a script I happen to have almost by memory. Each time I see it in the theatre I am always 'caught' in the performance in such a way as to have to make choices involving decisions about character or situation. The choices are always open because there are always alternatives. Let me cite just one example. At the point where Isabella is requested by Marianna to beg Duke Vincentio to spare the life of Angelo, Isabella's attempted rapist, I am always moved to choose for myself what should be done: I always want to see Angelo executed for his crime. In some productions I have even heard an inner voice chant directions to the Duke: 'Kill him, kill him, kill him . . .'. But then, of course, I do not get my wish: Isabella succeeds in her appeal and, as the Duke rescinds the order of execution, Angelo is dragged kicking and screaming into the necessary responsibilities of life. There are at least two points of interest here: first, the character's choice to beg for her attempted rapist's life, and secondly, my response *at that moment* as part of an audience. The second point of interest is the one that most fascinates me, particularly in relation to David Mamet's drama, because he often uses similar points of open choice to take us through a process of participatory discovery, and further understanding through reflection.

Mamet is extremely forthright about his art. He has written well and clearly on dramatic theory, which will help us not only with his own plays but also with the example of *Measure* mentioned above. He returns to three specific areas in his writing on drama: the actor, the subject and the audience. He says that the successful actor's 'performance will be compared not to *art*, but to *life*; and when we leave the theatre after his performance we will speak of *our life* rather than *his technique*'.[3] So, if *Measure* is acted well (and for the sake of argument let us say that it has been), then the response to which I referred above is really related to my life and not to false or cheap 'tricks' of the acting. Mamet is very concerned with skill in acting learned through practice and study:

This is what can and must be passed from one generation to the next. Technique – a knowledge of how to translate inchoate desire into clean action – into action capable of communicating itself to the audience. This technique, this care, this love of precision, of cleanliness, this love of theatre, is the best way, for it is love of the *audience* – of that which *unites* the actor and the house: a desire to share something which they know to be true.[4]

Here is one of the cornerstones of Mamet's dramatic theory: theatre is the unity of actor and audience in search of truth. Notice how the stress is, refreshingly and unusually, upon the act of communication to us as an audience. But what is that truth and what does it tell us?

Mamet clearly knows what it is not, and he indicts a great deal of contemporary American drama for presenting that which is not true:

> To the greatest extent we, in an evil time, which is to say a time in which we do not wish to examine ourselves and our unhappiness; we, in the body of the artistic community, elect dream material (plays) which cater to a very low level of fantasy. We cast ourselves (for in the writing and the production and the patronage of plays we cannot but identify with the protagonist) in dreams of wish fulfilment.[5]

Such subject matter has no salutary effect; it merely gives us what we want, and we learn nothing. 'We leave the theatre after such plays as smug as after a satisfying daydream. Our prejudices have been assuaged, and we have been reassured that nothing is wrong, but we are, finally, no happier.'[6] So plays must not be purely wish fulfilment; they must be more, and for a very specific reason: because wish fulfilment will not make us truly happy. Again, the emphasis is on the effects created on an audience.

In an extremely useful piece entitled 'Radio Drama', Mamet articulates other essential elements of his theory.

> To be effective, the drama must induce us to suspend our rational judgement, and to follow the *internal* logic of the piece, so that our *pleasure* (our 'cure') is the release at the end of the story. We enjoy the happiness of being a participant in the process of *solution*, rather than the intellectual achievement of having observed the process of construction.[7]

Although Mamet is writing about the experience of a play as a whole here, 'process' is one of the key words: it insists on the fact of a time continuum and it involves the audience directly in that continuum as a participant. 'He has said that the theatre is a place in which intent and will can be celebrated, and that no subject is a fit subject for drama which does not involve a possible choice.'[8] Choice is thus an absolute necessity, both from the point of view of character and, by extrapolation, from the point of view of the audience. But the experience of the choice is a fleeting one because the 'magic moments, the beautiful moments in the theatre always come from a desire on the part of artist *and* audience to live in the moment – to *commit* themselves to time'.[9] Again, Mamet is articulating a theory based upon audience participation in the temporal experience of drama, but this is not to say that a commitment to time necessitates the impossibility of analysing that moment we live in, as Mamet himself fully realises: 'the theatrical experience must be an *adoration* of the *evanescent*, a celebration of the transient nature of individual life (and, perhaps, through this, a glimpse at some less-transient realities)'.[10] Those 'less-transient realities' are nothing less than the truths he claims as the object of the commitment of actor and audience. Even though the moment is evanescent, the critic can keep faith with Mamet by freezing that moment in time through memory, which is one way of demonstrating how we leave the theatre reflecting upon our world.

So, to take the simple Shakespearean example above, my wish to see Angelo dead tells me nothing about the character; rather, it tells me a great deal about myself when faced with the possibility of the implementation of forgiveness or even grace in the face of what I find most appalling. When my choice is 'wrong' – when the logic of the play dictates that Angelo must live, rather than die as I wish – the experience of the moment forces me into a recognition or a remembrance of my morality in my world, which is exactly the opposite of wish fulfilment. In Mamet's terms, drama fulfils its proper function: 'The theatre is not a place where one should go to forget, but rather a place where one should go to remember.'[11] The participant who reflects is then led on to questions of further exploration. Who am I to decide issues of life and death, particularly when the 'victim' herself disagrees with me, or on what basis do I make my choices at the moment I make them? Every participating member of the audience undergoes a similar experience. In short, we leave the theatre talking about ourselves and our relation to the moral world in which we live. The point is that the 'play' is not posing an abstract question about mercy or justice; it is putting us in the position where we must *make* choices in a particular moment,